SOUTH AUSTRALIA

Books by Michael Page

Novels
Spare the Vanquished
The Innocent Bystander
Magpie's Island
A Yankee Skipper
The Seizing of the Brig
All in the Same Boat
Fortunes of War
A Nasty Little War

Australiana
*Fitted for the Voyage: The Adelaide Steamship Company
    1875–1975*
The Flying Doctor Story 1928–1978
South Australia
Riverboats and Rivermen (with William Drage)

Travel
A Sea With Many Islands

For Children
The Runaway Punt (with Robert Ingpen)

SOUTH AUSTRALIA

compiled and written by
MICHAEL PAGE

RIGBY

PHOTOGRAPHERS

The photographs in this book were taken by the
following:
Steve Berekmeri
Jocelyn Burt
Peter Finch
Jim Gully
Doug Luck
Publicity & Design Services, Premier's Department
SAPFOR Australia
David Wilson

See page 104 for individual acknowledgments. All
photographs are copyright.

Frontispiece: 'Light's Vision'. Adelaide's skyline photographed
from the statue of Colonel Light, who laid out the city in
1836, on Montefiore Hill, North Adelaide

National Library of Australia
Cataloguing-in-Publication entry

Page, Michael Fitzgerald, 1922–
   South Australia.
   Bibliography.
   ISBN 0 7270 0939 7
   1. South Australia—History—1834–1977.
   I. Title.

994'.23

RIGBY LIMITED • ADELAIDE • SYDNEY
MELBOURNE • BRISBANE • PERTH
First published 1979
Copyright © 1979 Rigby Limited
All rights reserved
Wholly designed in Australia
Printed in Hong Kong

Contents

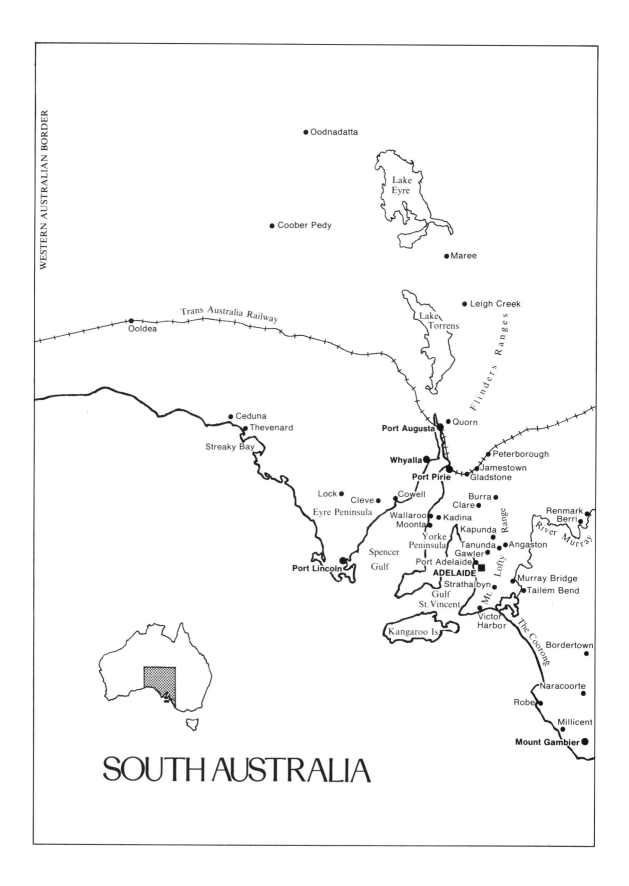

WESTERN AUSTRALIAN BORDER

● Oodnadatta

Lake
Eyre

● Coober Pedy

● Maree

Trans Australia Railway

● Leigh Creek

Lake
Torrens

Flinders Ranges

Ooldea

● Ceduna
● Thevenard

Streaky Bay

Quorn
Port Augusta

Whyalla

Peterborough
Jamestown
Gladstone

Port Pirie

Lock ● Cleve ● Cowell
Eyre Peninsula

Burra
Clare

Renmark
Berri

Wallaroo
Moonta
Kadina

Kapunda

Range

River Murray

Yorke
Peninsula
Spencer
Gulf

Tanunda
Gawler

Angaston

Port Lincoln

Port Adelaide
ADELAIDE

Lofty

Murray Bridge
Tailem Bend

Strathalbyn
Gulf
St. Vincent

Mt.

Victor
Harbor

The Coorong

Bordertown

Kangaroo Is.

Naracoorte
Robe

Millicent

Mount Gambier ●

SOUTH AUSTRALIA

1

Heart of a State

"The object is not to place a scattered and half-barbarous colony on the coast of New Holland, but to establish . . . a wealthy civilized society." Such was the ambition of the men who planned an English colony upon new principles.

Their ideas had been implanted by Edward Gibbon Wakefield, who had attacked the system under which Australian land was sold. Sometimes this was for as little as 1s 6d an acre. Wealthy settlers could purchase enormous tracts, but, since the labouring classes could not afford to emigrate, the landowners were obliged to hire convicts to work the land.

Wakefield believed the Crown should sell colonial land at more realistic prices, and use the money to assist migration. This would "cost less than maintaining the paupers in their parishes at home," and create communities balanced between well-endowed landowners and the respectful toilers whose passages they had subsidised.

Wakefield's theory found fruitful soil in the England of 1830. As so often, England was fermenting with new movements and ideas — and with the revolutionary spirit

caused by the poverty which followed the Napoleonic Wars. The first Reform Law was being hammered out, and such personalities as William Wilberforce had striven to awake her social conscience. It was the seminal period of the great era of evangelism, self-help, and social reform.

The idea of sending the parish poor to the New World was not a novel one. Mr Robert Gouger, one of the earnest gentlemen who were much concerned by the state of their nation, saw 200 emigrants taking ship for America at the expense of their Norfolk parishes. Wakefield's theory offered the method by which many others could be helped in the same way, but Gouger's first attempts were unsuccessful. His Emigration Society and National Colonisation Society both collapsed, partly because he could not decide on the site for a colony.

Then he read of the explorations of Captain Charles Sturt, who had traced the Murray River down from the Darling-Murrumbidgee river systems to the coast of South Australia. Sturt wrote in his report that: "A spot has at length been found on the south coast of New Holland to which the colonist might venture with every chance of success, and in whose valleys the exile might hope to build for himself and his family a peaceful and prosperous home."

These glowing words reawakened Gouger's ambitions, especially when a party of emigrants asked for his advice. But he was frustrated by the Colonial Office, and the emigrants grew so tired of waiting that they departed for America instead.

Despite further setbacks, he persisted. In 1834 he inspired the foundation of the South Australian Association, with himself as secretary and George Grote as treasurer. Such influential men as the Duke of Wellington looked favourably upon their efforts, and on 15 August 1834 the royal assent was obtained for "An Act to empower His Majesty to erect South Australia into a British province." The phraseology has enabled several generations of pedants to insist that South Australia was never a colony, but a province of Great Britain.

Wakefield, who had a natural interest in this first fruiting of his theories, wanted its yet-unbuilt capital to be named Wellington, but King William IV wished it to be named after his consort, Queen Adelaide.

The Act was a blueprint for a colony such as Wakefield had envisaged. South Australia was to be an independent province administered by a Board of Commissioners, which could sell its land for not less than twelve shillings an acre and use the money to establish an Emigration Fund, for the purpose of "conveying poor emigrants from Great Britain or Ireland to the said province . . . who shall as far as possible be adult persons of the two sexes in equal proportions, and not exceeding the age of thirty years." The Act also stated that no convicts should be transported to South Australia, so the province developed into the only State without roots in convict labour.

The Commissioners could borrow £250,000 to establish the province and pay the passages of the first emigrants, but Clause XXIV stated that "no part of the expense of founding and governing the said intended colony shall fall on the mother country." Before the Commissioners could begin their work, they had to sell land to the value of £35,000, and invest £20,000 of this amount in a special bond issue.

This provision nearly aborted the scheme. Gouger and his friends found it hard to sell land in a virtually unexplored colony. Advertising, public meetings, and personal salesmanship failed to sell more than half the required amount, until a capitalist came to the rescue of the theorists.

He was George Fife Angas, a wealthy Scottish merchant who had taken a philanthropic interest in the scheme and had been appointed one of the Commissioners. He told the Commission that the only answer was to form a Company and sell shares to the public, so that moneyed citizens could take a profit without going to the trouble of emigrating.

His proposal caused such outraged demands as, "Is this philanthropy, or business?" to which he calmly replied that it was both. With his friends Smith and Kingscote, he put down £9,000. Much argument followed between the idealists and the capitalists, but in October 1836 George Angas and four directors formed the South Australian Company, which offered shares at £50 each to buy South Australian land and use it for building, leasing, selling, wool-growing, farming, and cattle-raising. The company would salt down beef and pork for export; engage in whaling, sealing, and fishing; lease houses, commercial buildings, farms, and pastureland to emigrants; and establish a bank.

Angas knew his business. Within four days he had sold £200,000 worth of shares, and had more than covered the necessary sale of land. The South Australian Act could come into effect.

Nowadays it may seem hard to believe that George Angas described this result as "the direct answer to prayer." Nevertheless such an attitude typified that of the founders of South Australia; men who believed profoundly in a just God who gave them responsibilities as great as the fortunes with which He had rewarded their hard work.

The promoters of the colonisation scheme also belonged to the South Australian Church Society, which pointed out the moral advantages of "conveying to the colony young men and women in equal proportions." As an offshoot of this, they foresaw that, "The proportion of children to grown-up people would be greater than was

Parliament House, North Terrace, was opened in 1889 but the building was not completed until the 1930s . . . and it still lacks the dome planned in the original design

ever known since Shem, Ham, and Japhet . . . the whole colony would be an immense nursery." In such circumstances, they would soon attain the population of 50,000 which would enable the Commissioners to surrender their administration to a representative government.

The establishment of South Australia as a community of free citizens caused rumblings from the colonies governed by the military and supported by convict labour. They believed it created a dangerous vacuum, and New South Wales squatters said the land price of twelve shillings an acre was absurdly high.

The first British colonists, including "divers of His Majesty's subjects, possessing among them considerable property," left England early in 1836. After five months at sea their vessel *Duke of York* anchored in Nepean Bay, Kangaroo Island, and as soon as the first party had landed on the beach they held a thanksgiving service led by the ship's master.

They were a serious and religious company of pioneers, both Methodist and Church of England, and from the very beginning intended that their province should be a different place from those under the bloody and inhuman role of the convict-masters.

A motley gang of settlers already lived on Kangaroo Island, so named by the navigator Captain Matthew Flinders because its kangaroos provided fresh meat for his crew. Sealers, whalers, and ex-convicts, with Aboriginal wives enticed from the mainland tribes, existed in squalid contentment under "Governor" Waller, and seem to have rubbed along pretty well with the new colonists.

Nine ships brought the settlers from England, and the names of a number of those who sailed in them are still preserved in Adelaide's streets and squares. The squares are named after John Hindmarsh, the first Governor; William Light, the Surveyor-General; W. Wolryche Whitmore,

Chairman of the Provisional Committee of the South Australian Association; and James Hurtle Fisher, the Resident Commissioner and Registrar. Besides those of Gouger, Wakefield, and Angas, the streets of Adelaide have such names as Jeffcott, after the first judge; Gilles, the Colonial Treasurer; and Gilbert, the Colonial Storekeeper. Sturt Street commemorates Captain Charles Sturt; Flinders Street is named after Matthew Flinders, who charted and named the coastline; and the Board of Commissioners is recalled by such names as Lefevre Terrace, Montefiore Hill, the River Torrens, Hutt Street, Mackinnon Parade, Palmer Place, and Wright Street.

Perhaps the most significant of these names is that of Colonel William Light. The son of an English officer and an East Indian lady, he had fought under Wellington in the Peninsula War and after various further adventures and wanderings had been recommended by the Iron Duke for appointment as the Surveyor-General. He arrived at Kangaroo Island in his little ship *Rapid* on 20 August 1836, drawn by the knowledge that he had to find a suitable site for a capital city before Governor Hindmarsh arrived in H.M.S. *Buffalo*.

He found the settlers busily engaged in establishing themselves in and around Kingscote, but dismissed the idea of placing the capital on an island. Moving as fast as though he knew that the tubercles which were consuming him would give him only three more years of life, he inspected possible sites along the mainland coast from Port Lincoln to Encounter Bay. When Hindmarsh landed on 28 December, Light had made up his mind.

That afternoon, Robert Gouger administered the oath to Governor John Hindmarsh, who issued a proclamation which included his "firm determination to punish with exemplary severity all acts of injustice or violence which may be practised or attempted against the natives."

But black and white soon came to grips.

Below: Government House, on the corner of North Terrace and King William Road, was built for Governor Gawler in 1840 at a cost of £10,000

Facing page: The world's largest collection of Aboriginal artefacts is housed in the South Australian Museum on North Terrace

The Milemnura tribe of the Coorong area massacred the survivors of the brig *Maria*, and were punished by hangings. The Battara, of the Port Lincoln district, were incensed by settlers taking their tribal lands, and by murdering some of them — including thirteen-year-old Edward Hanson, who tried to fight off a war party singlehanded — began a guerrilla warfare which dragged on for years.

Most savage were the so-called Rufus tribe, of the upper Murray. Their attacks on overlanders of sheep and cattle made the settlers send three punitive expeditions against them, each of which they defeated. But Major O'Halloran's police expedition at last settled their hash, "with great slaughter." The Cowandilla tribe, of the Adelaide area, simply faded away, and the State's estimated Aboriginal population of 12,000 had fallen to 3,763 by 1903. Since then it has risen again to about 6,000.

The swearing-in of Governor Hindmarsh was followed by a mild celebration, of which one writer recorded sourly that, "A dozen or so drunken marines from H.M.S. *Buffalo* discharged several muskets in honour of the occasion." Of more significance was the thump of a printing press, set up on the beach and turning out copies of the pro-

clamation. From its first moments, the colony had the means of communication.

Hindmarsh, who was a retired Navy captain with strong ideas as to his own importance, soon decided to take his staff for a walk to inspect the site which Light had chosen for the new city.

Light had selected a position on the gently undulating plains which slope down from the Mount Lofty Ranges to the sea. They appealed to him because they were crossed by the narrow Torrens River and by five almost parallel creeks, which promised a permanent water supply, and because, "A more beautiful spot can hardly be imagined . . . with thousands of acres of the richest land I ever saw."

The beauty of the plains was enhanced by the hills from which they descend, and which nowadays form the background to the city. Before houses had begun to climb up their lower slopes, and before so many trees had been cut down to feed the cooking-fires and build the early homes of Adelaide, they must have been lovely indeed.

"The enchanted hills," Light called them, and some hint of that enchantment can still be found in deep, still gulleys dense and redolent with bush. They have been carved away by quarries, pierced by roads and a

Below: Ayers House, North Terrace, was once the home of Sir Henry Ayers, financier and politician. Now it contains assembly rooms, a restaurant, a bistro, and the headquarters of the National Trust of S.A.

Facing page: Adelaide's largest department stores all stand on Rundle Mall, which is reserved for pedestrians only

freeway, bitten into by housing estates. But enough remains to hold Adelaide in an amphitheatre formed by the ranges curving away to north and south; green and cloud-fogged in winter, lion-coloured in summer, hazed in red-gold light at sunset. The citizen of Adelaide can always "lift his eyes unto the hills."

Hindmarsh admired the serene tree-clad plains, which one of his staff said had "A fine old English look," but said bluntly that the site was too far from the sea.

Such nautical arrogance did not sit well with Light. When Hindmarsh made alter-native suggestions, Light insisted that he alone had the responsibility of situating the city. The consequent battle divided the settlers and caused the recall of the Governor. But Light won, and the city of Adelaide is laid out on the site he chose and according to the plans which he drew. It is one of the few cities of the world to have been com-pletely planned before one brick was mortar-ed to another.

Light's plan made use of the two plains which are divided by the broad, shallow valley of the Torrens. Adelaide itself is sited on the southern plain, and joined to the suburb of North Adelaide by King William Road and the City Bridge. He drew a plan which made the city a mile square, sur-rounded by 930 hectares of parklands. These were to separate the city from its suburbs, and, despite sequestration of some 240 hec-tares, they do so to this day.

It is unlikely that Light foresaw the growth of the city of Adelaide to such an extent that its metropolitan area now sprawls far beyond the parklands, but present citizens have cause to bless his foresight. The park-lands mean that the city itself, the centre of commerce and administration for the State, has grown up free from the mass of semi-slums and minor industries which besiege most other city centres.

South Australia has been described as "the driest State of the world's driest continent," and the parklands provide grateful vistas of green lawns and shady foliage and seem to allow the city to breathe. They have been vastly improved during the last twenty years, before which the parklands suffered, like so much of South Australia, from lack of water. In summer, like the rest of the State, large

areas of parkland withered into a parched brown.

The vigorous development of the State's water resources enabled an equally vigorous programme of parklands improvement. Considerable portions which once were almost wasteland, grazed upon by bakers' horses and dairymen's cows and profusely decorated with empty wine and beer bottles, have been landscaped, grassed, and planted with thousands of young trees and shrubs which are growing up proudly amongst the longer-established plantings.

Pleasant touches such as the model boats pool in the West Parklands, the canoeing lake in the East Parklands, the Alpine Res-taurant in the South Parklands, and Ben-jamin's Restaurant, in the North Parklands, have added to their attraction. There are huge stretches of well-kept turf, many fine groves and avenues, and a number of grassed or hard-surfaced sports areas which come into strenuous use in the evenings and on Saturdays.

Best of all is the fact that the parklands provide an almost pastoral peace in a city which like all others is in thrall to the auto-mobile. On a summer morning you may stroll across soft grass, through the great pools of shade cast by ancient gums and well-developed exotics, past shrubberies loud with birds and flower-beds proud with blooms, along ornamental waters brushed with weeping willows, and almost forget the clamorous rivers of metal fighting down their bitumen beds.

Amongst the longest-established portions of the parklands are the Elder Gardens, sloping down to the Torrens Lake to the west of King William Road. Beyond them is what must surely be a unique feature in a city of 917,600 people: a scenic and tree-adorned golf-course which is less than ten minutes from the city centre.

Standing at Adelaide's busiest intersection, that of North Terrace and King William Street, you look through and across trees to the spire of Saint Peter's Cathedral, standing lofty and dignified beyond the century-old Adelaide Oval and the Torrens Lake. The "cathedral end" is well-known to listeners to Test Matches broadcast from the Oval, whose turf has been trod by every well-known cricketer from Grace to Hobbs,

Above: This serene stretch of Torrens Lake, the haunt of many waterbirds, is only a few minutes from the city centre. The building is Benjamin's Restaurant

Below: This picnic area in Rymill Park, in the East Parklands, is an example of how the parklands surrounding the city have been developed for recreational use

Bradman to Benaud. In winter, it is raucous with the crowds who come to relish the gladiatorial combats between the Magpies, Tigers, Double Blues, and other football teams.

That stretch of the Torrens which flows through the Elder Gardens was once the city's main water supply. It came racing down out of the hills in winter but sank to a string of muddy pools in summer, with naked youngsters swimming and cattle drinking next to the watercarts being filled, and so it was a fine source of infection and animosity. When the first city water supply was laid on from the Thorndon Park Reservoir, in 1860, the citizens' thoughts turned to more ornamental uses for the Torrens. In 1881, it was dammed by a weir, and the Torrens Lake was created.

The lake is a handsome stretch of water for a city in which rain may not fall for many months at a time, and as well as pleasing the eye its surface supports pleasure boats and the racing shells of school crews, who compete annually in Henley-on-Torrens. Both lake and river have been improved during the parklands programme. Stretches of the river which once were eroded rubbish dumps have been prettily integrated into the parklands, and people are beginning to forget that the name of Pinky Flat has nothing to do with the flowers which grow there nowadays but originated with alcoholics who drank cocktails of wine and metho amongst its reeds.

The Torrens Lake now possesses the Elder Fountain, a soaring spire of illuminated water which is one of several fountains established in the city during recent years. They rest the eyes of shoppers dazzled by sunbaked streets and provide amusement for students who fill them with coloured detergent.

Colonel Light's critics said that his plan for the city was "nothing more than that of a military cantonment." It is true that his gridiron design has a certain martial rigidity. It consists of four main streets, Morphett, King William, Pulteney, and Hutt, running almost exactly north and south and passing through five equidistant squares, of which the broad plateau of Victoria Square stands in the centre of the city.

These four streets are connected by nine which run east and west, and a number of smaller parallel streets and "places" link

these together. The whole city, which rises to the flattened crest of one of the undulations of the plain, is surrounded by the four terraces which have the blunt names of North, South, East, and West.

This angular design, and the elevation of the city, has one great advantage. You can stand almost anywhere, on any street, and your view will not be interrupted by buildings. You can look south along King William Street and see the hills around Blackwood framed in the poplars of Victoria Square, or look north to the tree-lined ridge of North Adelaide. Raise your eyes from the crowds of Rundle Mall, and you see the hills again. Though some may feel that Colonel Light's design is somewhat mechanical, and that it has forever forbidden the delights and mysteries of winding lanes and unexpected nooks to the people of Adelaide, it has nevertheless given them these broad and spacious vistas.

The terraces around the city were favoured residential streets to begin with, because of their views across the parklands. They are still favoured in this way — especially East Terrace, which unlike the other more disciplined terraces moves in dips and curves. But West Terrace has become a traffic artery, and many of the fine old homes of East and South Terraces have become advertising agencies, offices, clubs, flats, or boarding houses, or have been knocked down to make room for used car yards, showrooms, and "town apartments."

North Terrace, perhaps, retains most of its original flavour. It is a fascinatingly bipartite street, devoted to commercialism on its southern side and to government, the arts, learning, culture and healing on the northern side. One of its most pleasing features is the trees which grow along it on either side, stretching, with various interruptions, for over a kilometre. Many of these are fine old plane trees, of which the massed foliage provides welcome summer shade.

North Terrace runs eastwards from its busy junction with West Terrace, where the noble colonial pile of the Newmarket Hotel looks down the Port Road towards the Thebarton Police Barracks. The Barracks contain a lecture room familiar to humbled motorists, and the stables of the splendid Police Greys, whose horses gaze mildly over the fence at

Above: Boating on the Torrens Lake, with the city and the Festival Theatre in the background

Below: Generations of South Australian students have passed over the University Footbridge, crossing the Torrens, on their way to the playing fields on the other side

model boating addicts around the pond in the West Parklands. South Australia has a very fine police force; efficient, physically smart, and well respected.

For the first few hundred metres, North Terrace is undistinguished. On its northern side are the railway yards, which probably are no worse than railway yards elsewhere. Its southern side is a somewhat drab array of commercial buildings and hotels, amongst which Trinity Church stands soot-smudged and forlorn. One of Adelaide's oldest churches, it looks very like an English parish church. It is overshadowed by Morphett Street Bridge, which carries one of the traffic arteries to the north.

From the bridge, you may glimpse the chimney of the West End Brewery, where for more than a century Yorke Peninsula barley and Tasmanian hops have been transmuted into a brew which loyal South Australians swear has no equal in the Commonwealth — if, indeed, in the world. Each year, the Brewery chimney is freshly painted in the colours of the football team which wins the Premiership.

Once past the railway station, North Terrace blossoms into the Old Legislative Building, which like so much of old Adelaide and its suburbs is solidly built of South Australian stone. Next to it stands Parliament House, said by some unkind people to be just like politics: marble in front for the voters to see, and plaster and brick behind. It was completed in the 1930s, though the cupola which was to balance its broad steps and massive pillars has never been placed on the squat roof. These two buildings stand as reminders of the day in 1851 when the colony took its first step towards self-government, and the first members of the Legislative Council took their seats.

Opposite, the multi-storey Gateway Motel arises where the elegant colonial pillars and verandahs of the South Australian Hotel once stood, now sacrificed like so many of the old buildings to the city's need to grow, like New York, upwards. It is near the

Bonython Hall, in the university grounds, is used for university ceremonies, concerts, and other cultural occasions. Sir Langdon Bonython laid the foundation stone in 1933

Above: The guardhouse at the entrance to Government House. The first Government House was only three wattle-and-daub rooms with a thatched roof

Below: The intersection of North Terrace and King William Road is one of the city's busiest crossings. The monument is to men of the Bushmen's Corps who served in the South African War, 1899–1902

huge A.M.P. building on the corner of King William Street and North Terrace intersection. East of this intersection, North Terrace comes into its own.

The Terrace's longitudinal division into culture and commerce, represented by its northern and southern sides respectively, in some ways typifies the atmosphere and background of Adelaide itself. The earnest businessmen who founded and developed South Australia strove just as vigorously to make their city into a moral and cultural community as they did to profit from its trade. Naturally some of their efforts foundered on the rocks of human wickedness. It is said that Coromandel Place once contained a thriving row of brothels.

But the merchants endowed much of the University of Adelaide on North Terrace and perpetuated their names in such buildings as Bonython Hall, the Elder Conservatorium, and the Barr Smith Library. They initiated numerous charitable organisations, such as the W. C. Rigby Cottages built by the bookseller who founded the publishers of this book, and the tradition which they began is continued by more recent benefactions. Their ideals may be scoffed at in this age of tax evasion, but nevertheless the city of Adelaide as it stands today owes much to the combination of capitalism and idealism first advocated by George Fife Angas.

The old homes once occupied by leading citizens have either disappeared from the southern side of North Terrace, to be replaced by office blocks, department stores, and parking stations, or have been converted to similar uses. Though the massive stone Adelaide Club still looks across at Government House, with its shuttered windows as withdrawn and discreet as the eyes of an old family lawyer.

It is balanced, towards the eastern end, by the stern Presbyterian edifice of Scots Church. Despite its commercial aura, however, the south side of the Terrace is still a pleasant boulevard, and returning travellers say wistfully how pleasant it would be if sidewalk cafes could be set out beneath its plane trees in the European style.

On the northern side, the sidewalks are even shadier, and there was a fearful outcry a few years ago when it was reported that the City Council planned to cut down the trees in order to widen the carriageway. Each councillor hastily denied that he had even thought of the suggestion. So far the trees remain, though it must be said that some South Australians seem to be tree-haters.

Cool spot on a summer day: the Lavington Bonython Fountain in front of one of the wings of the South Australian Museum

East Wing of the Royal Adelaide Hospital, North Terrace. One side overlooks the peaceful Botanic Garden, which contains more than 5,000 specimens of tropical and sub-tropical plants

The North Terrace trees are part of an almost continuous garden which runs from King William Street to Frome Road, and provides a green haven for office workers who litter it with their sandwich papers. This garden runs between the sidewalk and the long stone wall of Government House — itself surrounded by a huge garden upon which the city planners are casting their greedy eyes — and then becomes a broad stretch of turf in front of the War Memorial.

Across Kintore Avenue, it continues all the way to Frome Road. It passes the South Australian Institute; the splendid new State Library; the Museum; the Art Gallery; the University of Adelaide; and the South Australian Institute of Technology. Here the Terrace crosses Frome Road, which swoops northwards through an avenue of enormous elms, and the gardens continue in somewhat more exiguous form in front of the Royal Adelaide Hospital until North Terrace meets East Terrace. Thence it continues eastwards

between the East Parklands and the magnificently planned and maintained Botanic Garden, which contains more than 5,000 specimens of tropical and sub-tropical plants.

Adelaide folk have a special affection for North Terrace. They beautify it on Flower Day by covering its turf with floral carpets and placing flower arrangements amongst its trees, and throng its sidewalks to see the unsophisticated Saturnalia of students on Prosh Day. They have seen their troops march down it in three wars, commemorated by the bronze trooper on the Bushmen's Memorial outside one corner of Government House gardens and the War Memorial on another. They have erected their statues upon it; of Flinders, Edward VII, Robert Burns, Sir Samuel Way, and the massive but discreetly shielded nudes beloved of the Victorians. They lined it to cheer the Queen, Prince Philip, and the Queen Mother. They plant poppy-crowned crosses in its gardens for men who did not return from such places as Beersheba, El Alamein, Kapyong, and Long Tan.

On the second Saturday in November of each year, they watch John Martin's Pageant mark the official opening of Christmas selling and celebrations. They flirt under the North Terrace trees, rest weary feet by its pool and fountain, lounge on its lawns, inspect the glass-covered beehive or the whale skeletons in glass cases outside the Museum.

Old men upon its benches break off discussions on things past to cast appraising glances at the girls who strut, sway, stroll, or stride along its footpaths; an eternal procession of young South Australians who seem themselves to be like a floral pageant, whose beauty is renewed annually like that of the trees under which they pass. The comfortable mum who with her children awaits a suburban bus was one of them not long before.

But the greatest attraction is the cultural complex which fills the great oblong bounded by North Terrace and Victoria Drive and by Kintore Avenue and Frome Road. Much of it is occupied by the University, whose older buildings have a gnarled and ponderous look somewhat reminiscent of Victorian pedants, but the many new buildings added during the last thirty years are more graceful and spacious, as befits an era which attempts to make education a gift to everyone instead of a privilege for the few. More slab-sided and functional are the newer buildings of the Institute of Technology, which gradually is being squeezed out by the University into a fine new home on the northern outskirts of the city.

This cultural oblong contains an astounding variety of buildings, arranged haphazard across the slope which runs down towards the river. They range from the simple stone buildings of the early settlers, built originally for such purposes as a police barracks but now occupied by offshoots of the University and Government departments, to the soaring tower of the Adelaide Teachers College, tacked onto the fake Spanish hacienda of its parent building. There are wooden "temporary" buildings crouching under the rear wall of the Museum. There is a theatre and an observatory; lecture halls and laboratories. The Art Gallery, like the Museum, holds collections of treasures of which many of the

Bert Flugelman's sculpture in Rundle Mall, erected in October 1977, is a great attraction for passers-by

populace are unaware, and from time to time has played host to exhibitions worth millions of dollars.

Much of the State's history is preserved in the Archives, beneath the spacious new State Library which has been tucked between and behind the old Public Library and the South Australian Institute. The Institute, once the repository of the State's cultural life and headquarters of a number of country and suburban institutes, is still the meeting place of learned societies. It is a pleasingly proportioned building with the simple lines of early colonial architecture.

For seven days a week and up to twelve hours a day, people flow across and along North Terrace and in and out of one or another of these buildings like bees fertilising their gardens of culture or seeking their honey of learning and enlightenment. Many of these people are young, but plenty of

Above: The Art Gallery of South Australia, on North Terrace, houses a splendid collection of paintings and other works of art and plays host to many exhibitions, as indicated by these displays during an Adelaide Festival of Arts

Below: Ancient and modern on King William Road. St Peter's Cathedral, with an interstate jet above it heading for West Beach Airport

cropped grey heads may be seen as well as the glistening hair of children and the gay hirsute elaborations of liberated youth. All of them contribute towards North Terrace's special atmosphere; eager, alive, forthcoming, and somehow vibrant with the power of the human spirit.

Such people are believed by those of other States to be "conservative" — even though Victorians used to send to Adelaide for books banned in their own cities, and South Australia's abortion law reform is reputed to have attracted travellers. In fact, South Australia has rarely lagged behind in political or economic progress.

One of the world's first agricultural machines, the Ridley Stripper, was built here in 1843. Government control of education has existed for 120 years, and two of the State's public schools, St Peter's and Prince Alfred's, are older than many wellknown British schools. South Australia was first to introduce the secret ballot at elections.

Women's liberation began in 1894, when they were given the vote. Women have been justices since 1915, and Australia's first woman judge, Roma Mitchell, was appointed to the State Supreme Court in 1965. The Real Property Act, which initiated the world's simplest and most secure method of transferring land ownership, was passed in 1858. The eight-hour working day has been law since 1873, and, in 1876, South Australia was the first State to recognise trade unions.

The *Advertiser* newspaper is decades older than many British and American journals. An Adelaide man, L. de Mole, invented the military tank. Adelaide G.P.O. housed one of the world's first telephone exchanges in 1883, Australia's first tramway ran from North Adelaide to Kensington in 1878, and what was then Australia's largest ship, the 62,000 tons *Amanda Miller*, was launched in Whyalla in 1971.

South Australia was ahead of the other States in the establishment of democratic ideas, and far outstripped the mother country. The secret ballot and full manhood

Below: The Victoria Square Fountain, designed and sculptured by John Dowie. The large aluminium figures symbolise the three rivers which provide Adelaide's lifegiving water: the Murray, Torrens, and Onkaparinga

Facing page: The GPO, once the tallest building in Adelaide, stands on the left, with the Town Hall diagonally opposite across King William Street

Carclew was one of the splendid mansions built in North Adelaide during the colonial era. Sold to the government, it became a multi-arts activity centre for young people in 1976

suffrage, which did not start in Great Britain until 1872 and 1884, were instituted in South Australia in 1856. Members of the South Australian Parliament began to receive pay for their services in 1887, twenty-four years before those of the "mother of parliaments." Women of Britain were not permitted to vote until 1918.

It is in any case a mistake to generalise upon the character of a community of 1,268,800 people, especially one as diverse as that of South Australia. At its base is the substantial foundation of white Anglo-Saxon protestants who settled the State, and have been added to continually over the years. They gave South Australia its stodgy but comforting traditions of English law, justice, and social responsibility, and have been enriched and enlivened by the gingery independence of the Irish and the sinewy individuality of the Scots.

In 1838 began the first of several waves of German migrants: Evangelical Lutherans

fleeing from religious persecution. These were followed by the Cornish communities which migrated virtually en masse to the successive copper discoveries at Kapunda, Burra, Wallaroo, and Moonta. They added Cornish pasties to the South Australian diet (though they would not recognise the meagre modern specimens) and such names as Polwheal, Tregaskis, and Penaluna to the Smiths, Macdougalls, O'Houlihans, and von Schellenbergs to be found on the electoral rolls.

These mainstreams of migration were accompanied by lesser rivulets, such as Spanish muleteers brought out to cart the copper ore from the mines to Port Wakefield; Afghans with their camel teams, to go swaying through the sand and scrub of the far north; and even some Chinese. Sym Choon's fireworks delighted generations of young South Australians, and one of the State's leading firms of consulting engineers is P. G. Pak-Poy and Associates.

26

Above: Spacious grounds and sweeping views make the Flinders University one of the most striking of Australia's modern universities. Founded in 1966, it stands at Bedford Park, south of Adelaide. The huge new Flinders Medical Centre occupies the same area

Below: Veale Gardens, in the South Parklands. W. C. D. Veale, Town Clerk of Adelaide 1947–65, played a leading part in the conversion of the parklands from open paddocks to pleasant gardens and recreation areas

Towards the end of the nineteenth century, when the Americans began to check the vast flow of migration to the U.S.A., those Europeans who wanted a better life began to look towards Australia. South Australia received its share of Italians, Greeks, Russians, and Poles, together with some Syrians and Lebanese. But it was during and after the 1940s that the second huge migration began.

First came the Estonians, Latvians, and Lithuanians who had suffered so cruelly under the Russians and Germans, and whose children are now handsome young South Australians. Then the British, and then, in swelling numbers, Italians, Greeks, Yugoslavs, Turks, Hungarians, Finns, Czechoslovaks, Scandinavians, Ukrainians, Dutch, Germans, Austrians, and others — including such 'stateless' folk as descendants of the White Russian colonies in China. A number of these migrants were assisted by the State and Commonwealth plans which are the lineal descendants of Wakefield's scheme.

Most of them stay, though some return to their homelands exuding wrathful disappointment. Besides the permanent migrants, a good many African and Asian students spend several years in Adelaide. The sight of a sarong or an Afro haircut no longer causes heads to turn on North Terrace.

Since 1945, all these migrants have added their own special savours to South Australian life, like sauces and spices to a sustaining but perhaps unexciting menu. Their influence has been aided by a community swing towards a more invigorating life style, hastened by such Labor government reforms as the legalising of lotteries, tote betting, and the extension of drinking hours.

Yet in some ways this movement has been no more than a reversion to Adelaide as it used to be. The pious founders of the city were not spoilsports, and "congregations of empty bottles" stood around the tents of the first settlers. They came, after all, from an England which still had the extrovert exuberance of the Georgian era. They relished every human pleasure from sex to snobbery, and built scores of public houses in Adelaide and its immediate environs. Staffed by full-bosomed barmaids, these were used for entertainments ranging from a caged tiger to boozy dinners and dances, and were as important to the community as the dozens of edifices which earned Adelaide its old name of "the city of churches."

But Prince Albert's priggish influence filtered out to the colonies, and the Canadian-born politician King O'Malley did away with the barmaids, and in 1915 the temperance societies won six o'clock closing. Most of the public houses remain — there are still eighty-six in Adelaide and North Adelaide — and having been solidly built of stone with the addition of balconies and verandahs ornamented with cast-iron lace, they offer prime examples of colonial architecture.

Now, they have taken on a new lease of life, and have been redecorated to conform with Adelaide's new image and to compete with the scores of cafes, restaurants, and motels which have been opened in the city and suburbs during the past few years. The *Advertiser* can run a regular feature advising its readers where to eat, drink, and be merry, which would have been a hard task for any journalist twenty years ago.

The quality of life has changed in other ways besides permitting citizens to enjoy discos, bingo, and public drinking at night. In 1966, when tear gas was added to the armoury of the South Australian Police, an *Advertiser* cartoon showed two bored constables watching the shopping crowds, with the caption, "Imagine them rioting, and us using tear gas on them." Since then, South Australians often have taken to the streets to air their feelings about many things from the war in Vietnam to uranium mining in Arnhem Land, although most of these demonstrations have comprised more sound than fury.

But such things are only one manifestation of the ideas and idealism flourishing in the rich topsoil prepared by generations of South Australians, and fertilised by money drawn into the State during the long and vigorous administration of Sir Thomas Playford. These ideas have many other forms, including the Adelaide Festival of Arts which since 1960 has attracted many internationally famous performers, and the new Salisbury Teachers College which has been described as "possibly the best in the world," and an increasing concern with the dispossessed.

Once, the more sophisticated South Australian tended to believe that greener pastures lay over the eastern border, but this tendency is being slowly reversed.

As always in changing times, many citizens are uncertain whether the changes are for good or ill. In the straight streets of Adelaide which parallel North Terrace, old buildings have tumbled to the wrecker and others are marked for doom. Such changes cause resentment, but many old Adelaide commercial buildings are ill-planned and undistinguished, and the towers of steel and glass can at least offer a more efficient use of city space.

Adelaide's busiest streets are those closest to North Terrace, and on the northern side of Victoria Square. The name of each street changes as it crosses King William Street. Rundle Street and Rundle Mall, which houses most of the big department stores, becomes Hindley Street, with its jumble of shops, picture theatres, pubs, cafes with a Greek or Italian flavour, and finally the West End Brewery.

Grenfell and Currie Streets and Waymouth and Pirie Streets are the boulevards of big business. Next come Franklin and Flinders, flowing from west and east into the northern side of Victoria Square. The G.P.O., once the tallest building in Adelaide, stands on the corner of Franklin Street, with the Town Hall diagonally opposite across King William Street. Both these buildings have clock towers, and by some unrevealed miracle of administration their clocks always coincide.

The attractive old Treasury Building, which has stood since the gold escort brought home the gold won by South Australian diggers on the Victorian goldfields, is opposite the G.P.O., and looks across the Square to the Watch House on the corner of Angas Street: the old police headquarters which somewhat resembles an opera house. It is within handcuff-throw of the Supreme Court and other judicial buildings.

Recent multi-storey erections have made the older buildings around Victoria Square look dull and shabby, and it is hard to appreciate the square's trees and gardens

The Regional Office of the Bureau of Meteorology, Kent Town, keeps an eye on Adelaide's very changeable weather. It can vary from 3 to 40 degrees Celsius throughout the year and drop 10 degrees within an hour or two

Above: This piece of 'cast iron lace' on a North Adelaide home is one of countless examples to be seen on South Australian buildings of the colonial era

Facing page: The Cathedral of the Orthodox Church of Archangels, in Franklin Street, Adelaide, is characteristic of many fine places of worship built by European settlers

because of the traffic which pours through it in all directions. A statue of Queen Victoria stands dumpily above the roaring stream, and those of the explorers Sturt and Stuart gaze over cars and buses as though seeking a way back to the silence of the inland. John Dowie's beautiful fountain, symbolising the rivers of South Australia and commemorating the royal visit of 1963, stands in the centre of the square.

Grote and Gouger Streets, running into the west of the square, offer the excitements of the Central Market and the Opera Theatre. The rebuilt market, with its multi-coloured aisles of fruit, vegetables, meat, fish, cheeses, flowers, and garden plants, is a theatre in itself.

The streets south, east, and west of Victoria Square hold many relics of the days when large families lived in their solid stone houses and cottages, attended their schools and churches, and were served from their numerous pubs. Many of the cottages are still occupied, often at exorbitant rents, but most of the larger buildings between Victoria Square and South Terrace have been converted for business enterprises and small industries, including a print-shop which occupies an old church.

Others are used for institutions such as the Salvation Army Home and the Y.W.C.A., and others again have been replaced by offices, workshops, St Andrew's Hospital, flats for incapacitated servicemen, and so on. The old pubs thrive, but as a residential area the district still leaves much to be desired although there is a gradual trend towards renovating some of the old homes as town residences.

Most of the people who work in Adelaide nowadays come in from the suburbs connected to the city by the long, teeming traffic arteries. Like most cities of the world, Adelaide is undergoing the process whereby people either live further and further away from their work or, as the metropolitan area

expands, find a living in areas which formerly were suburbs or even farmlands.

North Adelaide, once a choice residential area, is a victim of this process, though some parts of it have been restored to fashion by a skilful restoration of old buildings, and there are still a number of streets in which fine old colonial mansions of the late Victorian and Edwardian eras have been kept in good repair.

Numerous large old homes have become doctors' rooms, and others have been replaced by high-rise flats, the splendidly-sited Hotel Australia, radio and television stations, and offices. Nevertheless the leafy streets and squares are still places in which the imagination can conjure up pictures of the days when life revolved around the Cathedral and Christ Church, and spanking teams of horses drew glistening equipages.

Rather the same may be said of all the older inner suburbs, in which homes from cottages to mansions were built between 1840 and 1940. Such areas present some sharp contrasts. The huge Highways Department building towers out of the quiet old streets of Walkerville. St Peter's College, opened in 1847, stands aloof in hectares of gardens and playing fields bounded by streets of gently crumbling houses. Warehouses, workshops, and the brewery's ugly grey malting kilns stand near Prince Alfred's College.

The ancient little homes of Bowden, on streets so narrow that two cars find it hard to pass and in which some garden walls are made in the old Devonshire style of clay and stones protected by a plaster coating, are overpowered by the gasworks. The neat 1920s villas of Colonel Light Gardens, product of the "Thousand Homes Plan" to meet a housing shortage of that era and administered by a Garden Suburb Commissioner, are now only a stone's throw from the growing commercialism of Daws Road and Goodwood Road. The expensive new homes built on the slopes of Shepherd's Hill look down on the Chrysler factory at St Marys.

Such "pretty little villages" as Norwood, Kensington, Enfield, Mitcham, Brighton, and Marion, whose pastoral occupations and little local industries once revolved around the city, have long since become city councils in their own right. Houses have encroached across the farmlands between them, to link all together in a suburbia which, as in any other metropolis, has social areas as sharply defined as Aboriginal tribal territories.

In the immediate area of the city of Adelaide, a rough rule is that the most desirable suburbs — and consequently the most expensive — are those which rise up the foothills to the east and spread along the coast to the west. The foothills suburbs have the advantages of elevation, especially at their southern end, and, at their highest elevation, the spaciousness granted by yet unbuilt-on slopes above them and the broad, tree-clad acres of the Waite Institute. The coastal suburbs have the beaches: a possibly questionable advantage when they are thronged by those seeking relief from hot summer nights or weekends.

In between these admittedly broad divisions there is a great variety of suburbs old and new, some with such evocative but no longer truthful names as Black Forest, said to have been cut down lest the Russians hide in it during the invasion scare of the 1870s; and Rosewater, which is in the general direction of the sewage farm and the hide and tallow works. Naturally they vary widely in quality, from the industrialised and semi-industrialised which run in a broad belt west and north-west of the city, and some well-planned newer suburbs, to the pleasant older homes of Unley, Fullarton, and Mitcham.

But the overall impression of Adelaide suburbs is that which may be given by the city as a whole: neat, rather houseproud, placidly content with present possessions but not averse to keeping up with the Joneses. The average South Australian is an obsessive gardener, a quality which gives many suburbs a leafiness and colour that helps to compensate for suburban councils who permit blatant advertising signs, cut down street trees with savage abandon, and do little to beautify streets rendered hideous by Stobie poles of steel and concrete (wooden ones are eaten by white ants) which support wrist-thick overhead cables. They have, of course, their excuses.

Architects and aesthetes deplore much that stands in the Adelaide suburbs, and certainly the raw and uninspired develop-

Above: A view across the plains of Adelaide, between its lovely hills and wide beaches (Photo: Jocelyn Burt)

Below: On a hot day in summer, hundreds of city dwellers flock to the Adelaide Swimming Centre in the North Parklands to enjoy the cool water and beautiful setting (Peter Finch)

Boating on the lake at Rymill Park, an area of parkland
developed in the early 1960s and now enjoyed by
many (Peter Finch)

Above: World artists visiting Adelaide are lavish in their praise of the Festival Theatre, overlooking the Torrens Lake flowing through the city (Jocelyn Burt)

Below: The gleaming white sands of the Port Willunga beach, only half an hour's run from Adelaide (Jocelyn Burt)

Left: These rugged cliffs near Flinders Chase, Kangaroo Island, once saw many shipwrecks. The Chase is now a famed flora and fauna reserve (Jocelyn Burt)

Above: Victor Harbor on the South Coast has the charm of an English-style beach resort (Peter Finch)

Above: Sunset shadows model hills near Willunga, south of Adelaide (Jocelyn Burt)

Below: Brownhill Creek in the foothills of the ranges circling Adelaide, an enticing spot for picnicking (Jim Gully)

A tranquil scene, Warren Reservoir on the South Para River,
built in 1916 (Jocelyn Burt)

Above: The narrow Morialta Gorge tucked between precipitous hills, a favourite challenge for climbers (Jocelyn Burt)

Below: The enchanting Mount Lofty hills bring bird life into the suburbs and even into the heart of the city (Jim Gully)

ment of large areas which can show nothing but endless variations on five rooms under a tiled roof is a saddening sight. Nevertheless there are many suburbs which look like one continuous garden, and reflect the endeavours of people who find their greatest contentment in home and family. This, perhaps, is the ethos of Adelaide.

But families have to be supported, and for many years now the population has been unable to live entirely upon the growing, getting, or processing of its primary products. The city and the State have during this century become an increasingly industrialised community, and now possess more than 6,000 factories producing a huge variety of products worth more than $3,460 million and employing almost thirty per cent of the work force. (Only about eight per cent of the work force is employed on the land, though the total value of rural production in 1976-77 was $705 million.) Mineral production in 1976 was worth over $131 million.

South Australian industries range from such massive organisations as The Broken Hill Pty Co Ltd, General Motors-Holden, Chrysler, Kelvinator, Tecalemit, and Philips Electrical Industries all the way down to workshops employing four or five men. But the local giants of industry prove that even the smallest factory may be germinating the seed of success, because many of today's principal producers grew from humble origins.

Simpson Pope, whose products wash the nation's clothes and cook its food, was founded by A. Simpson, who in 1855 set himself up as a tinman in Gawler Place. Sir Barton Pope began by making garden sprinklers. James Alexander Holden, whose name is now borne by hundreds of thousands of "Australia's own cars," was a saddler and ironmonger. John and David Shearer, founders of two firms of agricultural machinery manufacturers, were Scottish blacksmiths. In more recent times, a young Hungarian named Charles Rothauser began to make various products when the war cut down supplies from overseas. Nowadays, his firm Caroma is amongst Australia's biggest manufacturers of plastic ware and has extended overseas.

Up to the second World War, a good many South Australian manufacturers still bore the lingering taint of "colonial wares." Anything imported, preferably from Britain or America, was automatically regarded as superior. But, during the war, a number of large armament factories were built at Finsbury, and as soon as the war was over Sir Thomas Playford and his government realised their value to the State.

Their space was used as a magnet to attract industries seeking expansion, and the Playford government was soon obliged to supply power and water to satisfy the growing needs of industry of many kinds. The power was developed from coal brought from the new Leigh Creek coalfields, and the water poured in through pipelines from the River Murray. During the twenty post-war years of Playford Government administration the face of the State was changed from agricultural to industrial, and the cherry-grower from the Adelaide Hills was largely responsible for the industrial wealth of Adelaide today.

A potter at work in The Jam Factory, St Peters. It is a government-sponsored craft centre which produces an individualistic range of handicrafts

Yet much of industry still depends upon the primary produce of the land: iron ore from the Eyre Peninsula, limestone from Rapid Bay, copper from Kanmantoo, gypsum from the Yorke Peninsula, salt from Dry Creek, and so on. And the State feeds itself from its own wheatfields, pastures, fisheries, orchards, gardens, and vineyards, with the addition of such tropical imports as tea and sugar. Agriculture and industry come together in numerous ways, as in the tanning of leather and production of leathergoods from the skins of the State's own herds, or soapmaking from their fat, and chemicals from their by-products. Wool, the stubborn old basic which despite manmade fibres is still the friendliest and most comfortable of materials, is the backbone of the State's textile industry; worth about fifty million dollars annually and known throughout Australia by such brand names as Onka-paringa.

Australia's leading wool merchants and processors, the firm of G. H. Michell & Sons, is sited in Salisbury, north of Adelaide, and is a prime example of the State's proclivity for developing big industries from humble beginnings. In 1870, the Cornishman George Henry Michell began a woolbuying and woolscouring business at Undalya, in the Lower North. He washed the wool in the Wakefield River, dried it in the sun, and prospered so well that he had to move to Adelaide in 1896. The plant which he established at Hindmarsh, and run by his descendants, developed into Australia's largest manufacturer of wooltops: the stage to which wool is brought before going to the spinners for making into yarn. The company also handles huge quantities of greasy, scoured, and carbonised wools, and grew so large that a move to new five-million-dollar premises at Salisbury was made in 1973.

From a concentration upon the processing of wool, the firm extended into growing its own, and is one of the few wool merchants in the world to raise its own supplies. The next and almost inevitable step was meat

The dome of the Russian Orthodox Church of St Nicholas (Abroad) brings a reminder of Mother Russia to South Australians. Completed in the 1960s, the church took seven years to build

Above: St Francis Xavier's Cathedral, in Wakefield Street, Adelaide, is the centre of Roman Catholic worship. Commenced in 1851, it took more than a century to complete

Below: These Cottage Homes in Stanley Street, North Adelaide, were built for the accommodation of the 'aged and infirm poor and for widows' between 1873 and 1886

Above: Birkenhead Bridge, Port Adelaide, was Australia's first bascule-type bridge. Completed in 1940, it cost £150,000

Below: Once known as 'Port Misery' because of its mud and mangrove swamps, Port Adelaide has been South Australia's principal port since the 1830s

production, and the raising of fat lambs led them towards the purchase of cattle stations and then into general agriculture including the growing of cotton, wheat, maize, and other cereals. Most of the company's products, including such items as sheepskin rugs, seat covers, and medical rugs for hospitals, are now exported overseas.

The industries established in pre-war days tended to group close to the railways, or along the roads leading to Port Adelaide: the "Port Misery" of early settlers who landed their chattels amongst its mud, mangroves, and mosquitoes. Like most seaports, it is a conglomerate of old and new warehouses, industries, offices, and homes, and holds many relics of the days when the clipper *Torrens* was the crack ship on the London-Adelaide run. Its winding channels have long since been dredged and disciplined into the Inner Harbour, where freighters berth, and the Outer Harbour, reserved for overseas liners . . . although, in this age of jets, the sight of a liner is almost as rare as a wind-jammer.

Port Adelaide and its environs have become part of Adelaide's suburban sprawl, and the big new West Lakes and Semaphore housing developments have taken shape nearby. And, now that the semi-trailer has stolen so much trade from ships and freight trains, industry is spreading further afield — especially to the south.

South Australians have punished their environment as vigorously as most other communities; unthinkingly in the past, when they swept the land clear of so much of its ancient forests and bushland; carelessly or by necessity in the present — though a Minister for Conservation and the Environment has been appointed and has made his presence felt. But some of the area immediately south of Adelaide is a sad sight for those concerned with the environment.

The South Road, as far as the bottom of Tapley's Hill and then again through what used to be the quiet township of Morphett Vale, has become a jerry-built jumble of service stations, supermarkets, used-car

Tankers from oil-producing regions, including Australia's own Bass Strait oilfields, anchor off Port Stanvac and pump their cargoes ashore through a submerged pipeline. The Port Stanvac refinery produces 70 per cent of the State's fuel needs

yards, and takeaway food emporiums. Builders have covered the gentle slopes with monotonous suburbs. At Port Stanvac, the needs of industry have fenced off the pleasant rocky beach on which families once enjoyed themselves.

It is only a matter of time before the seaside resorts of Christies Beach and Port Noarlunga, with their fine broad beaches and sand dunes, become part of this commercialised suburbia. The process is well under way, though an attempt to exploit the area around Hallett's Cove was checked, temporarily at least, by protests from various bodies. The public concern it aroused was a promising sign that South Australians have seen the writing on the ecological wall.

But, further south again, the houses thin out and the South Road runs through farmland on its way to Victor Harbor. It links McLaren Vale, where some of the State's finest wines are produced, with the old township of Willunga, the centre of the largest concentration of almond orchards in the southern hemisphere. In late winter the mass of almond blossom causes the plains to glow with a pale rosy radiance.

This area is known as the South Coast, and its beaches attract those who seek even more space than is offered by the seven miles of "city beaches" between Brighton and Semaphore. From Port Noarlunga to the beautiful bay of Sellicks Beach the coastline is of low, soft cliffs, rich in fossils, and at Port Willunga they are topped by a strange formation of rhythmic clay domes. Beyond Sellicks it becomes rougher and rockier, in a jigsaw pattern of coves, beaches, and promontories as far as Cape Jervis. Many of the South Coast beaches — Maslin's, Port Willunga, Aldinga, Sellick's, Myponga, Second Valley, and Normanville in particular — have little communities of holiday houses and permanent homes.

Maslins Beach was the first beach in Australia officially declared open for nudists, and thus it may be seen as an example of the liberating effect of the government headed by Donald Allan Dunstan.

Don Dunstan, as he is always known, was born in Fiji of South Australian parents. They sent him home to be educated and he studied law at the University of Adelaide, practised in Fiji for a while, and then settled in his home State.

As a young lawyer and later as a Q.C. he became renowned for his passionate defence of underdogs and unpopular causes. He joined the Labor Party because of a dedicated belief that the lives of average Australians needed improvement in countless different ways.

Sir Thomas Playford's Liberal-Country Party government fell in 1965, and the ironical fact is that he was defeated because he had done so much to industrialise the State and attract many bluecollar workers who inevitably voted Labor. Shortly after Labor's accession to power its members voted Don Dunstan as their leader and Premier of South Australia.

Dunstan, then in his early forties, began immediately to liberalise the South Australian lifestyle. The famous 'pink shorts' episode, in which he attended Parliament clad in shorts and shirt instead of conventional attire, was a kind of demonstration of his intent to sweep away the cobwebs. Crusted conservatives turned purple, but many people began warily to sniff the winds of change . . . and to find them invigorating.

Dunstan's administration extended drinking hours from six to ten p.m., reformed the abortion law, instituted a State lottery to raise money for hospitals, opened official betting shops, and acted in many other ways to revise the laws governing life and labour in South Australia. A number of their reforms were soon followed by other States. At the same time, Dunstan's personal interest in the arts did much to open up new cultural vistas in South Australia.

He seemed to have a flair, intentional or otherwise, for attracting publicity of which the greater part was favourable. Possibly this is because the average politician is so drab by contrast with this colourful and controversial figure, who never hesitated to say exactly what he thought, often in words that cut like a scalpel, upon any State or national issue. The media was delighted to record his activities which ranged from poetry readings to the publication of his books *Don Dunstan's Cookbook* and *Don Dunstan's Australia*.

South Australians showed what they thought about Don Dunstan by returning his government to power again and again, until his retirement in 1979.

Naturally some of his reforms offended churchmen and others concerned with community morals, and his decision to allow nude sunbathing and swimming on Maslins Beach offended those who believe there is something intrinsically wicked in exposing the human pudenda.

Nevertheless it is pleasing in some ways to see countless men, women, and children naked in the summer sun: tanned, relaxed, and healthy. It is less pleasing to those who deplore the fact that great crowds have thus been attracted to a previously quiet beach, and to others who believe the old saying that 'One naked woman is beautiful. A hundred are just ridiculous.'

The coastal communities are linked by a road which separates from the South Road south of Noarlunga. It switchbacks over rolling country, swoops around the steep curves of the coastal hills south of Sellicks, turns inland to run through the pastoral downlands of Myponga and down into the steep valley of Yankalilla. Then it drives on over the steep undulations of the coast-line to Delamere and the crest of the ridge which slopes down to Cape Jervis and over-looks the rocky cliffs of Kangaroo Island.

A by-road leads down to the trim stone houses of Rapid Bay, named after Colonel Light's survey vessel. They are occupied by those who work in the limestone quarries or on loading the ships at its curving jetty.

Kangaroo Island lies across the mouth

Maslins Beach, first in Australia to be officially declared open to nudists, attracts many sunlovers (and spectators) in the summer months

39

of the Gulf of St Vincent, and its rocky cliffs can be seen clearly across the thirteen kilometres of water which separate it from Cape Jervis. This strait, called Backstairs Passage by Matthew Flinders, cuts the islanders off from the mainland in many ways. They complain that they do not receive their share of benefits which go to mainlanders as a matter of course, particularly in the case of education. For a young islander to continue he education, he must be sent to the mainland.

About ten years ago it seemed that Kangaroo Island would be even further isolated. For many years the steamer *Karatta* served the island on a regular run from Port Adelaide, and when this ship was scrapped her place was taken by the new roll-on roll-off vessel *Troubridge*, on a regular trade to the island and Port Lincoln. But passengers tended to go by air instead of sea, and bulk cargoes were insufficient to keep the vessel employed, so there was talk of cancelling the service. A private ferry venture, running from Cape Jervis to the island, was suspended at about the same time, and it seemed for a while that the only contact with the mainland would be by the daily air services — which would send up even higher the cost of goods which have to carry the transport charges and make it virtually impossible for the islanders to buy such items as cars, furniture, and farm implements. The impasse was broken when the Government decided to buy the *Troubridge* in order to maintain the service.

Kangaroo Island, which is 145 kilometres

Below: Willunga House, Willunga, is a pleasing example of colonial architecture. It was built in 1850 for Mr Malpas, the local postmaster, and recently has been lovingly restored

Facing page: The rhythm of the bouzouki is heard at Victor Harbor when thousands of Greeks assemble for the annual Greek Festival, one of the State's many ethnic festivals

Above: The seals at Seal Bay, Kangaroo Island, once attracted American sealers who killed them for fur and oil. Now they are one of the island's many tourist attractions

Facing page: A hang glider swoops above one of the spacious beaches and stretches of rugged cliffs which typify the coastline south of Adelaide

long and varies in width from only 1.6 km near Pelican Lagoon to fifty-five kilometres at its widest point, is the third largest island off the Australian coast after Tasmania and Melville Island. Its steep cliffs rise more than 200 metres in some places, and in the sailing-ship era were the graveyard of many craft.

Before the white man came, the island was uninhabited except for such wildlife as the kangaroos, which were so tame that Flinders' crewmen could knock them on the head and feast on their fresh meat. Its rocky shores abounded in seals, which attracted American sealers. Some of them built a ship at the entrance to Pelican Lagoon, subsequently called American River for that reason. Now, one of the island's holiday resorts stands nearby.

The tourist trade is one of the mainstays of the island. You can stay in the hotels or holiday shacks at Kingscote, Penneshaw, and other places, or purchase a package tour which covers return air travel, and an all-inclusive stay at one of the holiday centres which offer a planned programme of entertainments. 540 square kilometres of the island are a national reserve under the name of Flinders Chase, and there is talk of making the entire island into a National Park. Some conservationists resist the idea, with the feeling that, if its large areas of privately-owned farmland become public property, they will be open to pollution, indiscriminate shooting of everything that moves, and the starting of bushfires.

The island is an ideal place for a quiet holiday. You have a sense of moving back at least thirty years because of the lack of traffic, the unhurried pace, and the great areas of the island where you will rarely meet another human being.

The mainland seaboard of the South Coast area is fairly rugged for a part of the world which has a comparatively gentle sea, for storms in the sheltered waters of the Gulf of St Vincent tend to be short though vicious.

The rocky cliffs are low, but the land behind them rolls steeply along the coastline in high, denuded curves, with deep gullies which send winter torrents cascading to the sea. Near Myponga, this configuration has enabled the building of a reservoir which looks like a lake beside the road.

Though most of this area is farmed, there is still an untamed quality about much of the country which stretches from the Gulf coast across to the Inman Valley behind Victor Harbor. The rhythmic hills along the coastline are repeated inland, and from high points you may look across them and see that much of the old dark bushland survives above the lower slopes cleared for pasture.

Away from the coast and the roads, it is still lonely country. It is easy to imagine the isolation of the early settlers. There is an aloof nobility about these hills; a sense that they revealed their true character only to those who chanted the Tjilbruke legend around the corroboree fires.

The South Road rolls through them after climbing the steep hill behind Willunga, and eventually descends to Victor Harbor. This resort, and Port Elliot a few kilometres south, stands on a bay which in Europe would be fabled for its beauty. Part of it is called Encounter Bay, because the French and British navigators Baudin and Flinders met there in 1802, and it is one of the

Holidaymakers on the inlet of the Hindmarsh River at Victor Harbor, one of the State's oldest and most popular holiday resorts

places which Hindmarsh suggested as a site for the capital. One of its little rivers bears his name.

But despite the building of breakwaters, the anchorages on this coast were always too exposed to be safe for sailing ships. Victor Harbor flourished briefly as a whaling station, with whaleboats rowing out to harpoon whales in the bay and Aborigines waiting to gorge themselves on the carcasses dragged ashore, and then blossomed again when it was reached by the railway. It became South Australia's most popular seaside resort. Excursion trains brought day-trippers from Adelaide, and the wealthy merchants built splendid summer homes.

Together with its function as a centre for the rich pastoral areas round about, such has been its occupation ever since.

More and more holiday homes have spread around Encounter Bay, the caravan parks are packed, and improved roads now make it easy to visit the once lonely beaches of Parson's and Waitpinga. These face the Southern Ocean, and a tumultuous surf breaks along their miles of gleaming sand.

Port Elliot, around its aptly-named Horseshoe Bay, was once the terminus of South Australia's first railway, horsedrawn from the river port of Goolwa. A carriage is preserved in Goolwa's main street, but the railway has long disappeared. From Goolwa

This 'tourist train' carries holidaymakers across the causeway from Victor Harbor to Granite Island

Happy Valley Reservoir, lying in serene hill country south of Adelaide, was opened in 1896 and is one of the State's oldest reservoirs

another road turns back to Adelaide, and one of its ramifications will take you through Strathalbyn. The broad wooded glen in which Strathalbyn lies, and the church spires standing above its old stone homes, make it look from the distance like a little town as Scottish as its name.

It is on the Murray River side of the Mount Lofty-Flinders Ranges system of hills, which stretch for about 1,000 kilometres from around Victor Harbor up to the usually dry shores of Lake Torrens. They are rather miniature mountains, because the highest of the Flinders Ranges, St Mary's Peak, is only 1,200 metres, and Mount Lofty, overlooking Adelaide, only 700.

The Mount Lofty Ranges, at the southern end of the system, cause and catch most of the precipitation from the winter south-westerlies, and have the creeks, rivers, and catchment areas which have enabled reservoirs to be built in and around them. These alone would justify Colonel Light's choice of site for Adelaide. And the conformation of the ranges, which separate the fertile coastal areas from the more barren interior, has to a large degree dictated the course of settlement — just as similar formations influenced the pattern of settlement throughout Australia.

As well as this physical significance, they have special historical and emotional meanings for South Australians. The Mount Lofty Hills and the Flinders Ranges are the most striking geographical features in the State, though they vary greatly in structure. The Flinders Ranges, especially north of Quorn, are craggy and spectacular. The Mount Lofty Ranges, especially around and south of the Barossa Valley, are fertile, well-wooded, and more homely in aspect, though their rounded shoulders and ridges can be very steep.

Myponga Reservoir, south of Adelaide, is part of the continually-developing water storage scheme essential for residents in 'the driest State in the world's driest continent'

South Australians took to the hills very early in their history. The first were landless men who cut timber for the growing city, and they were followed by the German refugees who gave their little town the name of Hahndorf, after the captain of the ship which brought them to freedom.

Others found that the hills were ideal for fruitgrowing, and orchards of apples, pears, peaches, apricots, cherries, plums, quinces, and figs began to cover the hillsides at Clarendon and Ashton, Cherryville and Cherry Gardens, Humbug Scrub and Coromandel Valley. The rich soil washed down into the valleys, at such places as Brownhill Creek and Piccadilly, nourished plump crops of vegetables.

Dr Rawson Penfold planted one of the State's first vineyards on the slopes facing Adelaide, and soon the neat terraces of vines for winemaking and fruit-drying began to flourish on sunny hillsides. The city's need for water caused some valleys to be sealed off for reservoirs; first at Thorndon Park, later at Hope Valley, Happy Valley, Mount Bold, South Para, Millbrook, Myponga, and Kangaroo Creek. Happy Valley is supplied by a pipeline driven through the hills from the Onkaparinga at Clarendon, and on a still day lies like a lovely mirror in the serene countryside which rolls down from Cherry Gardens to the sea.

For four decades in the middle of last century, settlers carved their little holdings out of the hills and dragged their produce to market down precipitous tracks. Then, at last, the railways were finished; winding their way from Adelaide around Sleep's Hill and up through Eden Hills and Coromandel, Blackwood and Glenalta and Belair, to National Park, Mount Lofty, Aldgate, and Bridgewater. This easy transport enabled wealthy commuters to build splendid summer homes in the hills, and allowed humbler folk to spend their Sundays in National Park or to flock in their thousands — as they still do — to the Easter Monday races at Oakbank.

Also, it opened up the ranges to more and more people who were willing to brave winter fogs and frosts for the pleasure of living all year round amongst hills and trees. The end result was inevitable. The hills villages within a few miles of the city have become outer suburbs of Adelaide, with more and more houses being compressed around commercial centres blatant with supermarket techniques.

Mount Barker, a handsome mid-Victorian township just off the main road to Melbourne, may undergo "planned development" into a city of 80,000. Crafers and Stirling, whose pretty churches and cottages once seemed almost smothered by the trees which grew so closely round them, now reverberate to the endless freeway traffic, and there is talk of re-zoning Stirling so that light industries may be established in the area.

Yet much of the old hills magic remains, even though trail bikes roar through National Park. Away from the main roads and the railway, numerous little townships follow the seasonal rhythm of pruning, ploughing, fertilising, and picking. Sheep graze steep pastures which slope through "pillared woodlands," and cattle browse around huge gnarled old gums. English trees planted against the dark backgrounds of the native forests break into gay leaf and blossom, and fade with a glory of autumn colours. And, as everywhere else in and around Adelaide, the gardeners are at work; planting trees and shrubs and lawns to soften the scars of new developments. Over thousands of hectares and hundreds of kilometres, over the ranges which roll rhythmically away into the hazy distance, there is a serenity which seems to be expressed by the liquid fluting of the magpies amongst the trees.

Kangaroo Creek Reservoir, on the River Torrens Gorge north-east of Adelaide, shown with its water storage running low at the end of a long hot summer

2
River and Border

Along the serpentine banks of the Murray River, more liquid in the form of wine and fruit juice is produced in any given year than flowed between them in the form of water during 1916. That was one of the years in which the Murray dried up.

Like many Australian rivers, it was of capricious habit. When winter rains and snows fell heavily up in the Australian Alps, the spring flush of the Murray would fill its billabongs and swamp the lowlands between Mannum and Wellington. When the sun parched moisture from the mallee plains, the Murray idled along like a great green snake between its low, steep cliffs, watched by the massive eucalypts that waited patiently for another flood. Its habits were of no consequence to anyone except the Aborigines, who lived on its rich bounty of callop, perch, mulloway, and cod.

When the first settlers arrived, they thought the river mouth might be the genesis of a port like Liverpool or Hull. But its entrance is too diffused amongst sandbanks and winding channels to be penetrated by ocean craft, and the short, brutal seas whipped up at its mouth can be fatal to small

vessels. It was to develop a different kind of port and shipping system, built round the paddle steamers which plied all the way from Goolwa, near the coast in South Australia, to Swan Hill and Echuca in Victoria.

Two tiny vessels, W. R. Randell's *Mary Ann* and Francis Cadell's *Augusta*, were the first to prove that the Murray could be navigated. That was in 1853, and they were followed by a fleet of sidewheelers and sternwheelers ranging from barges with engines to elegant, colonnaded craft with soaring smokestacks.

A few, in various states of preservation, still remain. The *Coonawarra* and *Oscar W.* still ply the river, the *Captain Sturt* lies aground at Goolwa, the *Marion* is part of a folk museum at Mannum. These, and some others, are sole survivors of a roistering age. Riverboat captains and crews developed the special skills needed to navigate a river full of snags and sandbanks, with as many S-bends as a road through the hills, and water levels that fluctuated almost daily. Some skippers boasted that they could steam their flat-bottomed craft over a heavy dew.

The churning paddlewheels helped to push settlement further up the river, and by the 1880s the Murray banks downriver from Murray Bridge held some thriving communities. In 1881, the government had begun to drain the swamps between Mannum and Wellington, and the reclaimed soil grew rich pastures. Settlers enjoyed a modest prosperity around shallow Lake Alexandrina, on Hindmarsh Island, and near Langhorne Creek — where one of the State's earliest wineries still flourishes.

At Mannum, John and David Shearer began making agricultural machinery, and invented Shearer's Patent Wrought Steel Plough and Cultivator Shares for the benefit of farmers ploughing soil still thick with tree roots and stumps. As a pastime, David Shearer planned and built Australia's first automobile; a steam car which took to the rutted roads in 1898.

In 1887 the first Melbourne Express steamed over the rail bridge built across the river and swamps at Edwards Crossing, from then on known as Murray Bridge. Building the bridge had been a Pharaoh-like task of sheer brute strength, because the mass of ironwork for 603 metres of spans and piers had to be dragged over the Adelaide Hills by bullock teams. For many years it was the only bridge across the Murray, and all other traffic had to cross by punts. (Camels 1d., elephants 2d., the list of charges ran at the Goolwa punt).

From around Murray Bridge and downriver to Goolwa, the country began to settle into the pattern which it holds today, fairly level land which grows rich lucerne pastures, vineyards, orchards, and vegetables. Landholders along the river use its water for irrigation. But further north, and especially in what are known as the River Highlands, life was not so easy. The tantalising river idled for hundreds of kilometres through low rainfall country, seemingly so poor that a sheep needed three hectares of it to live on.

Alfred Deakin, Premier of Victoria, found the key. He persuaded the Canadian brothers George and William Chaffey to leave their irrigation colony in California and have a look at the Murray in Victoria. George Chaffey saw that while Mildura sheep station was perishing from drought, its homestead garden was growing fine fruit and vegetables in red soil irrigated from the Murray.

Deakin persuaded the Chaffey brothers to accept his offer to begin an irrigation colony at Mildura, but the Victorian Parliament hesitated to confirm it. The South Australians promptly offered the Chaffeys a grant of 12,000 hectares of land around Renmark, under a contract which obliged them to spend £300,000 on irrigation works but gave them almost unlimited land rights provided that they spent £1 an acre on settling the area.

An old building in Currie Street, Adelaide, demolished a few years ago, once bore in faded letters the words CHAFFEY IRRI-GATION COLONIES. The sign was still fresh when the grandiose scheme went broke, but during the ten years in which the Chaffeys struggled to make it work a community of settlers had been attracted to the Renmark area. In 1895 the pumping machinery and irrigation works were taken over by the Renmark Irrigation Trust, which virtually governed the area until 1960.

The State Government took a hand in irrigation schemes in 1909, and when returned soldiers were settled on the land after the two world wars. Originally, irrigation schemes followed the age-old technique of pumping water out of catchment areas into channels, but nowadays many orchards are hazed in mists of moisture as water is forced through sprays.

Irrigation has its problems as well as its benefits. The water soaks into the soil and must be pumped or drained into evaporation areas, but it also finds its way back into the Murray and carries fertilisers, pesticides, and mineral salts into the river. Some gloomy South Australians claim that they can taste them in the Murray water which is now pipelined into city and township supplies. Some orchards can no longer use overhead sprays because the water is so salty that it withers the leaves.

Despite the teething troubles of the irrigation colonies, they attracted a stream of "blockers" like a minor goldrush. City folk with a few pounds put by, farmers from the Adelaide Hills, and British families seeking a new life overseas were all tempted by forecasts that the red riverbank soil would grow them a fortune. To begin with they lived under conditions as primitive as on any goldfield, and as late as 1909 the river townships were described as "mostly wood and

Channel irrigation in the vineyards along the Murray River. The irrigation schemes literally have 'made the desert blossom'

Above: Souvenir of the days when the Murray lands were first opened for irrigation: an irrigation pump designed by George Chaffey who with his brother William was the pioneer of irrigation in Australia. The pump was built in 1892 in Birmingham

Facing page: Cable-drawn punts have carried travellers and their vehicles across the Murray since the pioneering days. This one is at Walker Flat

iron." Total abstinence was the rule under the Chaffey reign, so sly grog shanties flourished, but early this century the Renmark settlers decided to drink with dignity and formed the Renmark Community Hotel.

It was the first of many co-operative ventures in communities which, by the sharing of Murray water, have literally "made the desert blossom." Deakin's dream, like that of the early settlers, has long since come true. 8,000 hectares of citrus orchards, and many thousand hectares of blocks growing peaches, apricots, sultanas, currants, wine grapes, pears, and vegetables, now stand along the river.

From the air, they form an angular belt in many shades of green between the river and its parched hinterlands. The principle of fair shares has been extended by the numerous fruit processing and winemaking co-operatives at Barmera, Berri, Kingston, Loxton, Moorook, Paringa, Ramco, Mypolonga, Renmark, Waikerie, and Cadell —

where young delinquents work on the prison farm. The river townships are no longer "bare, unfinished, and dusty," but are as green and handsome as the well-tended orchards which surround them. Their principal problem, nowadays, is the cost of labour for picking, packing, and transporting their produce. Many of the smaller river farms are finding it difficult to survive.

While the first steam pumps were sucking at its waters, the river still followed its ancient habits. Sometimes the pumps sucked in vain; sometimes the river waters swirled around their fireboxes. So in 1915 the River Murray Agreement was made, and a quarter-century later the ancient giant had almost been tamed. The Hume Reservoir, above Albury in New South Wales, catches the first flow and holds it in a gigantic dam. Lake Victoria, just across the border, has been made into a catchment area for the irrigation settlements.

Five locks and weirs have been built across

the river, and five barrages across its outlets to keep out the Southern Ocean. Now, the river level has been raised — with the consequent death of thousands of river gums which have been "drowned," and stand white and stark along its edges. It remains fairly constant, though in 1956 the great river showed its contempt for man's works by a flood which caused great damage and several months of anxiety.

There are no river dams in South Australia but the Murray waters are vital to the State. South Australians are profligate users of water, especially in their gardens, and their industries require an enormous amount. Successive governments have supplied the demand with many water schemes which include the Morgan-Whyalla pipelines, running 359 kilometres to supply the steelworks and shipyards at Whyalla, and the pipelines from Mannum and Murray Bridge to Adelaide. "Do we drink *that*?" an aghast schoolchild once exclaimed on an excursion to the river, and the taste, smell, texture, and biological properties of South Australian water are the subject of much acid comment. Nevertheless the Murray water is the lifeblood of South Australia. Ninety-six per cent of the State receives less than fifty centimetres of rainfall a year, and even the comparatively well-favoured coastal belt has suffered from prolonged droughts.

Between the Murray and the sea lies an irregular triangle of land of which the upper portion is the Murray Mallee and the lower is known as the South-East. The Mallee was so named by the early settlers because in those days it was a seemingly endless sea of mallee forest, so dense that the first cart tracks were like tunnels through the slim, closegrowing trunks and the masses of foliage which glisten like water in the sun.

The low, wiry trees almost defeated the first settlers. Each mallee has several slim trunks growing from a hard, gnarled root, and cutting them one by one was an interminable labour. They solved the problem by breaking them down with huge rollers dragged by bullock teams, then burning the snapped off stems and grubbing out the roots. These too were burnt until the building of the railways across the Mallee, from Tailem Bend on the Murray to Pinnaroo and Peebinga close to the Victorian border, and to the irrigation settlements, enabled mallee roots to be sent to the city as fuel.

The land thus gained varied in quality from loose sandy soil to rich red flats between loamy ridges, but it is moistened by only about thirty centimetres of rain a year. The farmers developed a technique of "dry farming," with the help of artificial fertilisers, and began to grow fair crops and pasture. Water was found by boring 75 metres or more, and soon after the first wheat had been carted out of the Mallee the settlers began to replace their first rough shacks with wood and iron homesteads, and to develop a social consciousness which made them change the name of Polly's Well settlement to that of Peake, and Wow Wow to Lameroo.

Some had given up in despair, but those who endured began to prosper. It had been undramatic and unglamorous pioneering, with a nubbled texture woven of toil from first light to moonrise, and a diet of tea, mutton, and damper, and the acridity of bodies which there was scarcely enough water to wash, and the counting of coins on horny palms to reckon up whether there was enough to last until the first brave spears of wheat came into ear, and buggy rides to worship in the tiny clapboard churches, where faith was restored in the eventual goodness of the Lord to those who cultivate His soil.

It is a faith which has been tried hard, many times, through droughts and depressions and similar setbacks over which the farmers have no control. Yet the Mallee has an atmosphere of tough resilience like that of the mallee tree itself, and its miles of rolling farmland in which the wheat silos stand like watch towers are a living memorial to the endeavours of the pioneers.

Further south, where the railway from the Tailem Bend junction now runs to Bordertown and Melbourne, life was even harder. The land stretched like a gently rolling sea of dwarf mallee from horizon to horizon, swept by the winds which made the settlers give the bleak name of Cold and Wet to the present township of Coonalpyn.

The railway driven through the scrub made life a little easier, and the towns of Tintinara, Keith, and Cooke Plains began to struggle into existence, but a considerable part of the area had a problem which was not to be

Above: Wheat silos at Lameroo, in the Murray Mallee, store some of the produce of this huge region which gave South Australian farmers some of their hardest challenges

Below: The graceful Blanchetown Bridge replaced one of the punts across the Murray River ... and speeded up travel considerably. The dead river gums were 'drowned' when river locks raised the water level

First step towards luscious cakes and buns—picking currants at Cobdogla, near Barmera on the Murray River

solved for many years. The earliest drovers to traverse the impassive wilderness of scrubland gave it the name of Ninety-mile Desert, and those who tried to settle there found that its soil was useless for cultivation. Wheat sown in it rarely came to ear; sheep grazed in the scrub developed the defects which, further south, were known as "coast disease."

The reason was not found until agricultural research had progressed into the laboratory, where scientists discovered that these soils were deficient in such minerals as copper and manganese. The addition of minute quantities, in the form of "trace elements" distributed amongst fertiliser, was sufficient to cure their reluctance to grow anything but native plants and grasses.

Soon after the second World War, the A.M.P. Insurance Society invested millions of pounds in helping settlers to clear and cultivate the Ninety-mile Desert. Now, it is part of the 3.2 million hectares of the Murray Mallee growing wheat, barley, and sheep.

The coastline of the Murray Mallee is the Coorong; the *kahrang* (neck) of the Aborigines who killed the *Maria* survivors. It might be described as the vermiform appendix of the River Murray, being one of the lagoons which the river formed as it sought a way to the sea. Just below Wellington, the Murray widens into shallow Lake Alexandrina, which is joined to reedy, bird-haunted Lake Albert.

The waters of Lake Alexandrina find their way into the sea through the complexity of islands and channels which bewildered Captain Sturt when he was searching for the mouth of the Murray; a breach through a narrow belt of beaches and sandhills running from near Goolwa to Tilley Swamp. Southeast of the Murray mouth, this is called the Younghusband Peninsula, and behind it lies the still, reed-fringed waters of the Coorong.

For aeons, this long, narrow lagoon received some of the overflow waters of the Murray, until the water conservation works

Pelicans abound along the Murray, on Kangaroo Island, and on the Coorong. A pelican was the 'hero' of the famous film *Storm Boy*, photographed on the Coorong

caused the supply to be constrained. Denied their regular flushing and revitalising, the waters of the Coorong are stagnating. The fish that once teemed in them are departing, and so are the waterfowl and fishermen who lived on the fish, though pelicans still make their bellyflop landings on the Coorong waters, and wild duck can still be seen.

The Coorong has a mystique cherished by those who love the wild freshness of its beaches and the subtle beauty of its wind-sculptured sandhills. Even the cars speeding towards Melbourne along the Prince's Highway, which runs along its mainland side, do not rob it of its spacious loneliness. Hermit fishermen in rusty little shacks, and city folk in search of peace and silence, relish the winding channels between its tiny islands and the wind-scoured beaches of the ocean side and the steep sandhills.

"Over the Coorong sandhills only the wild ducks fly," Dorothea Mackellar could write in 1910, but nowadays the sandhills some-times have to absorb the uproar of trail bikes, outboard motors, water skiers, beach buggies used by illegal shooters, and the hovercraft of the Wild Life Department trying to find them. An angry letter to the *Advertiser* mentioned that obscene words had been lettered across the sandhills, and soft drink cans lie amongst the natural debris of driftwood, seaweed, and seashells. The mystery still remains for those who can sense it, but it is becoming increasingly hard to find.

Colin Thiele's famous book *Storm Boy*, one of the steadiest Australian bestsellers of the past twenty years, has the Coorong as its background. The South Australian Film Corporation went on location on the Coorong to make their film of the book in 1976. It has been the most successful Australian film of recent years.

The Coorong ends near the point where the Murray Mallee becomes the district known as the South-East, but most of the coastline to the Victorian border is of very much the same type. There are scores of miles of lonely beaches, backed by sandhills or by low limestone cliffs which have been carved into fantastic formations by the wind and sea. Limestone and sand are prominent features of the coastal areas, with the stone cropping up through the sandy soil or holding brackish ponds and lakes of which the largest are Robe, Eliza, St Clair, George, and Bonney, separated from the sea by the same kind of sandhill country as the Coorong. This belt of limestone, in some places, prevented water from draining into the sea, and caused much of the South-East to be reedy, swampy country further inland. Part of it was named Dismal Swamp by the pioneers.

This coast gives a feeling of immensity; of huge plains rising and rolling away inland; of seemingly endless beaches and sandhills. It can be a coast of fury in the winter, swept by bleak south-westerlies which wrecked many ships in the days before it was charted and lighted, and a coast of fire in the summer. Waterless, parched by the sun and the sea winds, its colour scheme is that of pale, dazzling sand and sombre scrub and bleached grasses.

It lacks natural harbours, yet the early settlers had to have outlets to the sea. They overlanded their stock into the South-East by plodding patiently through the scrub and fighting off marauding Aborigines, and when the homesteads had been built from scrub timber and limestone blocks they began to look for ways to send their wool-clips to market. The natural route was by sea, so that the clipper-ships could carry wool direct to Europe, and in 1846 the Government clipper *Lapwing* brought Governor Robe and the Deputy Surveyor-General in search of seaports.

For want of better harbours they recommended Lacepede Bay, on which the port of Kingston South-East was to develop, and the comparatively sheltered bight of Guichen Bay where Cape Dombey gives some protection from the gales. The town and port of Robe soon sprang up in the broad depression between the cliffs and sandhills of the cape and the low hills rolling northwards. Later, the ports of Beachport, Port Macdonnell, and Rivoli Bay were established further south.

All these ports have exposed, dangerous anchorages. Jetties were built so that wool could be lightered out to the clippers, and stores and settlers landed for the newly-opened districts, but shipmasters had to be wary of sudden shifts of wind. In 1862 the wool ships *Alma* and *Livingstone* became total wrecks near Robe, and added their timbers to those of numerous vessels driven ashore along the coast.

Nevertheless the South-East ports became vital channels of trade. Bullock waggons lumbered down from inland, highpiled with woolpacks, and lumbered back again with furniture, provisions, and knick-knacks for the flourishing stations. Some of the items which they purchased are still preserved in Robe's private museums, and include a Patent Snake Bite Cure which consists of a clumsy hypodermic needle and a vial of ammonia which was to be injected into the vein containing snake venom.

During the 1850s, Robe became a fashionable summer resort as well as a seaport. The summer Government House was built there — and still stands — and families made the sea voyage from Adelaide in search of refreshment from the heat. Whiskered gents and crinolined ladies were entertained by watching shiploads of Chinese coolies landing on the beach, and trotting off with pigtails bouncing towards the Victorian goldfields, a good 400 kilometres away. They preferred the journey through the scrub to paying the head tax charged in Victorian ports.

Like the other South-East ports, Robe flourished. While the roads were nothing but rutted tracks winding through the bushland, and the first iron for South Australian railways was still being forged in Scotland, the sea offered the fastest means of travel. Coastal ketches, schooners, and steamers anchored near the wool clippers, and as the inland towns developed and the settlers' bank accounts expanded the seaports became holiday towns for farmers and their families as well as for city folk. A "Coffee Palace" was built at Beachport, and men gnarled with a couple of decades of toil on the land lay in the Pool of Siloam, hoping that its salt waters would ease their aching joints.

But railways and semi-trailers have long

Above: The Customs House at Robe preserves some of the memories of days when Robe was a thriving seaport, shipping out the produce of the South-East

Below: Lake Butler, at Robe, was converted into a haven for fishing craft by excavating a channel which connects it with the sea

since taken the trade away from the sea coast, and the vessels in the South-East bays nowadays are mainly those of the fishermen. Off Robe, they catch the crayfish which are processed and packed in the S.A. Fisheries Co-operative plant to be shipped off all over Australia and overseas, and at various places along the coast young men in wet suits dive for abalone which will be sent to America.

These are seasonal occupations, and when crayfish are out of season or a bad spell of weather is expected the Robe crayfish boats are sailed through an artificial channel into one of the South-East's coastal lakes. There they can lie safely, watched by the ramshackle old Government House which has seen more than a century of nautical fashions come and go.

The old stone houses of Robe, and its Customs House and warehouses and the Caledonian Hotel, preserve many memories of the days when the first settlers were hacking properties of baronial extent out

of the immensities of the South-East. Like the other old ports it is still a popular summer resort. The summer homes of wealthy South-East farmers and graziers are scattered around them, and their miles of shining beaches are washed by sea of the same clean, brilliant blue as the sky. There is a feeling of space which makes an absurdity of gloomy predictions as to the world soon being too small for the people in it.

The first settlers, who came from British farmlands neatly apportioned since the days of the Doomsday Book, had the same feeling. "There's land galore for me!" one of them is supposed to have cried, and gleefully named his station Galore. The Fraser family settled on 8,000 hectares near Kingston, and William Miles built up a property of the same extent near Millicent.

Michael White, whose Irish parents took him to the South-East as a boy, joined with three others in purchasing and subdividing 48,000 hectares around Millicent, and another Irishman, Thomas McCourt from

Naracoorte, one of the townships of the South-East, stands in country which once had a problem unusual in South Australia: too much water. Surrounding swamps were drained by a complex system of channels

This old homestead stands near Keith, in the South-East, and is typical of the peaceful farms which for more than a century have raised wheat, barley, and sheep

Tyrone, battled through such adversities as losing 21,500 sheep from lung worm. He became the owner of 12,000 hectares.

The pioneers raised sheep, cattle, and horses, and prospered despite the depredations of Aborigines, wild dogs, and rabbits. As ever, the "land galore" proved insufficient, and settlers began to study ways of using land which was denied to them for a reason unusual in South Australia: that of too much water.

The South-East corner of the State does comparatively well for rain, and for aeons it had been falling upon the peculiar land formation in which a series of limestone ridges run parallel to the sea with "flats" or low valleys of soil between them. Trapped by the ridges, the water had created swamps which dried in summer but flooded in winter. It was said that stock grazed upon them needed webbed feet.

The solution was found by government surveyors and engineers, who in 1863 blasted a channel through the ridges in the Millicent area. 45,000 hectares of land were drained during the next few years, and the government and landowners have been draining the land ever since. A variety of schemes were employed, but the entire project is now under the control of the South-Eastern Drainage Board. Nearly 20 million dollars have been spent on draining the South-East since 1863, and about 1,500 kilometres of drains constructed. They can be seen everywhere, from the broad channels running down to the sea to the shallow ditches crossing broad paddocks, and the motorist who drives through the South-East will find that he is continually crossing bridges. 500 have been built across the drains, and the work of looking after them and keeping the drains in good repair is reflected in the landowners' rates.

But for many of them, for many years until the current agricultural depression, it has been a good investment. Inspector

Tolmer, who struggled with his men of the Gold Escort to find a way through the South-East swamps for the drayloads of gold sent home by South Australian diggers on the Victorian goldfields, would not recognise the South-East nowadays. The whole area reflects the work and lives of generations who have cherished the soil, and in many cases have built fine homes and planted beautiful gardens as the nuclei of their rich farms.

Most of the large towns of the South-East developed in about the same era; Naracoorte was first settled in 1850, Millicent in the 1860s, Mount Gambier in 1854, and so on. Penola claims to be the oldest, since it was founded by Alexander Cameron in 1840 and developed as a stopping place for those making the weary overland journey from Melbourne to Adelaide.

The area may have the richest of all the rich soils of the South-East; a deep red loam which prompted John Riddoch to found the Coonawarra Fruit Colony in 1890. He subdivided 404 hectares of his Katnook Estate into four hectare blocks, and sold them for fruit-growing and with the notion of founding an ideal community.

The fruit trees grew well, but the vines did best of all. The soil and climate are ideal for winegrowing, and the rotund clarets and burgundies of the Coonawarra vineyards are items on the South-East's list of good things to eat and drink. The fertile soils spread a gargantuan annual banquet; thousands of tonnes of potatoes and onions and other vegetables; silos full of wheat; succulent beef, pork, and lamb; butter and milk as rich as the South-East pasturelands; a galaxy of fine cheeses.

The South-East has been the larder of the State since the 1860s, when some of the earliest steamships to ply along the coast brought its potatoes and other produce to Adelaide.

The whole area has the self-respecting placidity of a community which lives close to the earth. Its towns have a pleasant maturity imparted by the ready availability of the white coralline limestone, known as Mount Gambier stone, and the red and grey dolomites, which enabled the builders of last century to erect imposing churches and public buildings. They stand beside the angularity of new schools and hospitals, and many trim homes reflect the prosperity of the last three decades.

Almost a century ago, the South-East was the site of a great experiment in acclimatisation. By the 1870s, enormous numbers of the trees which once flourished in South Australia had been destroyed, and in any case the State grew very little timber that was suitable for general carpentry. Most building and joinery timbers had to be imported, and the government established a Woods and Forests Department to remedy the situation.

The department recommended that softwood forests should be planted near Mount Remarkable, in the Upper North, and in the South-East. The trees chosen for propagation were the *pinus radiata*, a Californian pine which grows in conditions somewhat similar to the South-East, and the *pinus insignis*. The first South-East plantings were made in the Mount Gambier area, and responded nobly.

The South-East once grew countless thousands of great eucalypts, and a good many still stand and add to the park-like aspect of many of the properties. While the little pine trees were growing, the centuries-old eucalypts were being cut down, partly for sawing into sleepers for the new railways, partly for fencing and other farm uses, and partly because they stood in the way of the plough. Most pioneers had little appreciation of natural wonders, and cleared away the trees and bushland as vigorously as they rid themselves of the Aborigines, wild dogs, and the great mobs of kangaroos.

But the pine plantings have replaced the lost trees, and huge blocks of pine forest now cover more than 90,000 hectares of the South-East. From the air, they have a soldierly rigidity; drawn up in green battalions stretching across hills and valleys and separated by fire and access roads.

On the ground, this soldierly neatness is even more pronounced. You can look along and down the ranks, each one dressed trimly to its neighbours and stretching away in vanishing perspective. Yet a stroll into their depths is an entrance into the mysterious world of the Brothers Grimm. There is a haunted stillness beneath the great dark canopy of boughs, and the sunlight filters through them in dusty golden shafts to be absorbed by the dense, soft mat of needles on the forest floor.

Such romantic notions have no place in the timber industry of the South-East. Like soldiers, the trees are nurtured towards death, and are scientifically planted, fertilised, and culled. The story goes that forest workers, many years ago, realised that one pine tree was growing far bigger than the others because its roots were feeding in the pit dug for kitchen refuse. After that they began to fertilise the whole forest — usually from the air, nowadays — and consequently the trees grow bigger and faster.

The pines can be seen in every stage of development, from the miniature forests of the nursery patches to the ponderous trunks of the mature trees. In the past, much of the wood was wasted. No use could be made of spindling trees culled out to give room to the others, and all branches and twigs were burnt. Unless a tree was big enough to be sawn into planks or boxwood,

it was useless. But nowadays, by a chemical process which protects them from rot and termites, the smaller trees can be used for fenceposts.

Other wood, unsuitable for milling, can be minced into chips which are crushed together into particle board: a light and easily worked material which has found countless uses in building and joinery. Woodpulping for paper, paperboard, and paper tissues disposes of further great quantities of timber. And every scrap of timber, down to the very sawdust, which cannot be used for making some saleable product, is fed into the furnaces of South-East power stations.

Despite the fairytale atmosphere in the depths of one of the great forests, you would look in vain for the woodcutter and his daughter. The whole industry is mechanised. The ring of axes has been replaced by the screaming buzz of power saws, which enable one man to fell and lop a tree in a matter of minutes—and to cut it off five centi-

One day these seedlings will supply Australia with timber for building and many other purposes. They grow in the nursery of Southern Australia Perpetual Forests Ltd at Mount Gambier

metres above the ground, so that very little timber is left to rot as a stump. A machine has been developed that resembles a pair of gigantic self-propelled scissors, which can snip off a smaller tree and clip off its branches with almost alarming ease. Seedlings are planted by a machine which digs a little hole, drops in the tiny tree, tamps the earth around it, and adds a dash of fertiliser. By such methods, 4,000 new hectares are planted every year to replace the constant culling and thinning of older plantings.

South Australian pine has become a popular building material. It could not be used in the past because the soft timber soon fell prey to termites, but these have now been foiled by the process which fills the wood fibres with a preservative chemical and also gives the timber an attractive greenish colouration.

South Australian timber may be, quite literally, Australia's fastest-growing industry. "The value of the pine plantations increases by $600 every second of the day," said a salesman, and, when you imagine each of 1,200 million trees adding a fraction to its growth, the figure is easy to believe. He was a representative of a firm which enables many South Australians to own portions of these pine forests — though the foresters would find it hard to show one of these individuals the particular segment which belonged to him. You can "buy" your portion by means of a covenant which gives you an interest in 660 pine trees. You cannot walk amongst them in proprietorial mood, but the profits which they earn, beginning with the first thinnings after ten or twelve years and continuing until the last trees are felled after thirty years, constitute the return upon your investment. It can be substantial.

Something like 40,000 South Australians

This stand of mature radiata pine, in the forests of Southern Australia Perpetual Forests Ltd, is about ready for felling in the process of 'timber cropping' which continues year-round in the South-East

Above: The old court house at Mount Gambier is now a museum. Mount Gambier, developed from 1855, was named after Admiral Lord Gambier by a naval officer who sighted the mount from the sea

Below: Magnificent red wines have been produced in these vineyards at Coonawarra Estates Winery, Coonawarra, in the South-East. The area is noted for its rich volcanic soil and ideal climate

are dependent on the timber industry, and a good many of them live in the South-East. A number live in the timber towns such as Mount Burr, which at 240 metres is the highest point in this gently rolling landscape. Max Lamshed, the South-East author, said that they have "almost an Alpine atmosphere," imparted by the tangy redolence of growing pines and sawn timber, and by the tidy little communities which live remote from the rat race. Their principal dread is fire, which can leap through resinous branches swaying in a hot northerly wind. Timber men have given their lives in fighting to save the forests.

The timber belt occupies a comparatively insignificant corner, in terms of area, of a State which covers one-eighth of the continent. North of Naracoorte, the prolific and hospitable territory of the South-East becomes sparser and more arid, along the border which stretches ruler-straight (except for a kink on the Murray) for 1320 kilometres from the ocean to Queensland.

Much of it, away from the railways and the highways, is lonely and silent: a land in which, on a still day, an approaching car can be heard for five minutes or more as it trails its plume of dust along the rutted roads. Even some of the railways are almost silent. Such tiny townships as Taplan, Nangari, Noora, Taldra, and Yamba do not even see one train a day, and for most of the time the permanent way shines quietly under the huge blue bowl of the sky.

North of the river, beyond the flats which have been made fertile by nearly a century of toil, there are no more towns. It is station country, settled late last century by families which lived an almost patriarchal existence on holdings to which they gave names like Gluepot, Canegrass, Hogback, Postmark, Morganvale and Woolgang. They knew an isolation undreamed of today, thought it may be sensed in the silence of seemingly endless distances which even in the full glare of sunlight are remote, melancholy, and aloof. On the other side of the border, this is the territory which has been given the wonderfully evocative name of Sunset Country.

Southend, in the South-East, typifies the seemingly endless beaches which provide spacious playgrounds for holidaymakers

3

Two Peninsulas

If various pressure groups had had their way, the capital of South Australia might have been sited on either the Eyre or the Yorke Peninsula, probably with disastrous results in either instance. Among the founding fathers there were those who, being prepared to believe the best of anything said about their new province, listened eagerly to the stories of a sealer named Gould. With nautical hyperbole he told them of the beauty and convenience of Yorke Peninsula: of its fertile soil, good harbours, and rich fisheries. At about the same time some of the supporters of Governor Hindmarsh were lobbying for the capital to be placed at Port Lincoln, on the Eyre Peninsula. They were vastly impressed by the fact that its harbour, Boston Bay, could "accommodate all the navies of the world in perfect safety in any weather."

Both groups ignored or were ignorant of the fact that the Yorke Peninsula has no rivers and in fact few watercourses of any kind except for winter-fed creeks, and that the Eyre Peninsula can boast only the Todd River. In any case they were baffled by Colonel Light's insistence on choosing his own site for the capital, and had to content themselves with taking sides in the ensuing uproar.

Its outcome did not entirely quell their enthusiasm. Some of the propagandists for Port Lincoln took up land there and laid out a town which had the proportions of a city. But citizens were few and far between, and the 'streets' were so little trodden that a youth murdered by Aborigines was buried in the middle of one of them before the mourners realised what they had done.

The Aborigines of both peninsulas took poorly to the idea of having their tribal lands sequestrated by people who had no conceivable right to them. The Battara tribe of the Port Lincoln area were particularly unimpressed by missionary efforts to give them the word of God in exchange. They harried both settlers and missionaries so ruthlessly that the latter were obliged to build a church with an upper storey to which they could retreat in the case of Aboriginal attack.

The guerilla with the Aborigines continued for a good many years on the Eyre Peninsula, and numerous stories are told of it —

especially that of the Waterloo Bay massacre, in which white stockmen are supposed to have rounded up an Aboriginal tribe in revenge for the murder of a white family, and driven them over the cliffs. More recent researchers claim that only one or two Aborigines suffered in that way, or perhaps even none at all. But it makes a bloodthirstily colourful yarn, and there is no doubt that settlers and their families were murdered by Aborigines, and that settlers and police troopers reacted in the customary way until the "problem had been solved" and the invaders could get down to the task of making a living out of the land.

This presented plenty of problems in itself. The vast wedge-shaped land mass of the Eyre Peninsula is as big as Tasmania, but considerably more arid and on the whole less fertile. As in the rest of South Australia, its most productive agricultural areas are mainly around the coastline and towards the south. Edward John Eyre, the explorer after whom the Peninsula was named by Governor Gawler, made two ventures across it, and reported that he had not crossed a single watercourse between Port Lincoln and Streaky Bay. But he persisted with his notion of finding a route to Western Australia, which the *Perth Gazette* dismissed with the comments that South Australians had, "... revelled in moonshine long enough. If we wish to see them we can soon find our way."

Nevertheless the idea of limitless tracts of land exerted its usual magnetic attraction, and pioneers continued to land at Port Lincoln, and later at such ports as Coffin Bay, Streaky Bay, and Ceduna on the West Coast and Tumby Bay, Arno Bay and Franklin Harbour on the Spencer Gulf. Like so many places on the South Australian coast, numerous Eyre Peninsula and Yorke Peninsula features were named by Matthew Flinders and recall his crew and their vicissitudes: Cape Catastrophe where a boatload of men was lost, Thistle Island after one of his officers, Coffin Bay after an Admiralty official, and so on.

Though they were settling on mainland Australia, the pioneers of both Peninsulas might as well have been living on islands. It is 643 kilometres from Port Lincoln to Adelaide by land, and 1280 from Ceduna. To

begin with there was not even a track along the spectacular ocean coastline, nor over the wave-like succession of rounded ridges which run down to the Spencer Gulf between Tumby Bay and Port Augusta.

Even when roads were formed through the scrub they soon became rutted and eroded. Until the roads were sealed, during the last thirty years or so, the greater part of the traffic to and from the Yorke and Eyre Peninsulas went by sea. Many small ports thrived along the hundreds of miles of coastline from the head of the Gulf of St Vincent to the border with West Australia, and a number of them had jetties which nowadays are used only by fishermen and holidaymakers. For more than half a century the "Gulf Trip," on which such steamers as the *Moonta* and *Minnipa* sailed from Port Adelaide to Port Lincoln, made a round of the Spencer Gulf ports, and returned home, was a favourite honeymoon or holiday tour for South Australians.

A fleet of coastal vessels, including the Port Adelaide ketches, once carried cargo and passengers to and from the ports on the Peninsulas and the West Coast. Wheat clippers loaded for Europe at Port Victoria on the Yorke Peninsula and at Port Lincoln. Now, the sea traffic is concentrated on a few principal ports, though a new grain port, Port Giles, has been created on the Yorke Peninsula. It has a jetty 650 metres long and can load ships of up to 40,000 tonnes burthen.

The other ports, except for the Broken Hill Pty Co Ltd's wharves at Whyalla, are mainly employed for shipping grain, and the long queues of farm trucks waiting to unload wheat or barley into the silos at harvest time are one of the sights of the Peninsulas. At Ardrossan, on the Yorke Peninsula, the queue was once twelve kilometres long.

The farmers dozing in the cabs of the trucks, or yarning in their shade as they wait their turns at the silo, look as tough and weatherbeaten as the mallee which grows beside the long, straight roads. Some of them are descendants of settlers who took up land in the 1840s and 1850s, and although life is a good deal easier now than it was when shepherds had to protect the flocks against marauding Aborigines it still breeds a rugged and self-reliant stock.

The Yorke Peninsula is shaped rather like

Salt pans at Price, on Yorke Peninsula, have yielded a rich harvest of commercial and industrial salt for many years and the industry still flourishes

a miniature Italy, though the foot upon its leg lacks Italy's elegant booted heel. Flinders is said to have been the first to notice its resemblance to a leg, and to have committed the pun of naming Corny Point, one of the excrescences on its foot.

You are never far from the sea on Yorke Peninsula, and its weather is oceanic. The fresh, changeable winds sweep across its low swells of land, which rise occasionally into rounded humps such as Mount Rat, and they sometimes blow savagely enough to flatten the barley, of which it grows more than any other area in Australia. It is excellent malting barley, well regarded by brewers. The sun which pours down out of the high, windswept sky ripens it into miles of waving golden stalks, crackling crisp as breakfast cereal, before the harvesters come to take off their heads.

As the first cultivators discovered when they had to hack great chunks of it out of the ground, the Yorke Peninsula consists very largely of limestone. In many places, depressions in the surface limestone collect water which oozes through soil heavily laden with salt. When the sun evaporates the water, these depressions become salt pans: glistening white or flushed with a delicate pink by a mineral held in suspension. In their bowls of jagged limestone, and surrounded by low, coarse scrub, these salt pans give an impression of aridity which heightens the dry, windswept atmosphere of the Peninsula, but they have yielded a rich harvest since it first became possible to ship out the mineral.

Farmers who were lucky enough to have such salt lakes on their land employed wandering labourers as salt-scrapers, and a company formed to exploit the lakes near Edithburgh and Yorketown, near the "ankle" of the Peninsula, paid good dividends for many years. The industry still functions, especially at Price on the eastern coast, but has dwindled in importance since the

69

Ruins of old copper mines at Moonta, where the roaring furnaces of the smelters faded into extinction during the 1920s

establishment of solar salt works at Whyalla, Port Augusta, and Dry Creek. Altogether, the State's salt industry produces half-a-million tonnes a year, about eighty per cent of Australia's requirements, and is capable of almost unlimited expansion.

The limestone cursed by the early farmers eventually became the foundation of an equally important industry. In the 1890s, David Miller of Adelaide sent two men to the Yorke Peninsula to burn the limestone into building lime, and they built a number of kilns on the coast from Stansbury to Ardrossan. The kilns provided hundreds of tonnes of lime, and the output increased when the executives quarrelled and one of them set up another kiln, at Wool Bay. He established Wool Bay Lime Ltd, which nowadays is one of Adelaide's largest firms of building suppliers. But the old days in which the phrase "dry as a limeburner's boot" was coined have been overtaken by the technological age. Mechanical handling deals with

the lime which is burnt in automated kilns near Stansbury and Port Vincent.

Dolomite, extracted near Ardrossan and used in steel-making, is the third of the Yorke Peninsula mineral resources which are of significance nowadays, and gypsum is the other. But for about sixty years such mundane minerals as salt and limestone were very small beer when compared with copper. Men who still recall those days speak wistfully of the pulsing activity of the Wallaroo-Moonta-Kadina complex of mines and smelters.

By the turn of the century they were pouring out 40,000 tonnes of copper a year, of such quality that "it was one of the six brands accepted by the French Artillery Department for the manufacture of cartridge cases for quick-firing guns." In an age which recked nothing of air pollution, the smoke, dust, and fumes billowed across the clear waters of Spencer Gulf from the copper smelters. For six days a

70

Port Vincent, on the east coast of Yorke Peninsula, is a favourite holiday resort very popular with yachtsmen

week, the arid plain around the three townships was turnultuous with men and machinery, and on the seventh day the miners went black-suited to their chapels to bellow Wesleyan hymns and suffer the castigations of their preachers for Saturday night sprees. "If you 'aven't been to Moonta you 'aven't lived," was the proud boast of the dour, devout, hard-working Cornishmen who toiled under Captain Henry Richard Hancock and his son Lipson Hancock. The rank of "Captain" was bestowed by Cornish miners on any leader set over them.

But the roaring furnaces of the smelters faded into extinction during the 1920s, and the abandoned mine buildings are a tourist attraction for holidaymakers who camp around Moonta Bay. The Yorke Peninsula is a favoured vacation area for people from Adelaide and elsewhere, partly because the string of little ports, active or otherwise, give a dash of seagoing excitement to the holiday colours of golden beaches and blue sea and sky.

The ports are not very far apart, and it is seldom more than forty kilometres from one coast of the Peninsula to the other. Even if you follow the low spine of hills down the centre of the leg you pass quite quickly from one township to another — and can divert to visit spots on the coast. On the east coast, you can begin at Ardrossan, where there are likely to be overseas ships alongside, then drive down to Port Vincent where racing yachts lie out in the bay. Next comes Stansbury, and then Edithburgh, which is a mere ruin of its former glory. Edithburgh was for many years a favoured excursion point for Adelaide folk, even as early as the days when trippers had to be piggybacked ashore at Salt Creek, and it developed into the principal port of the Peninsula. Massive stone homes, warehouses, and churches were built there and still remain, but the port has a neglected and bypassed look nowadays even though ships still call there.

Above: The *Ethel*, in Ethel Bay on Yorke Peninsula, drove ashore in 1904 ... but vandals wrecked her more thoroughly than the sea had done

Facing page: Loading wheat at Edithburgh, now a mere shadow of its former glory as the principal port on Yorke Peninsula

It is an interesting and attractive spot for a visit, and you can cool off in the swimming pool at the foot of the low cliffs. The sea runs in and out of it over a barrier of rocks.

Edithburgh is on the heel of the Peninsula's foot, which protrudes into the strait that Flinders named after his ship *Investigator*. Its stormy waters are challenged by a harsher coastline than the rest of the Peninsula, and the countryside is more rugged than further north. Part of it is being preserved as Innes National Park, on the tip of the foot, and near here can be seen the wreck of the *Ethel* in Ethel Bay. She was driven ashore in 1904, and more recently a Greek ship came to grief in Stenhouse Bay.

The instep of the foot is marked by Corny Point, much favoured by those who enjoy a rough-and-ready holiday, and then as you begin to climb the western side of the leg you look out across some dazzling seascapes framed by long curves of low limestone cliffs which sometimes look almost golden in the sunlight, and are washed by seas which pass through an infinity of variations on sapphire, emerald, and amethyst. The water feels as good as it looks, and has a brilliant clarity so far unsmirched by pollution ... though an ominous note was struck a few years ago when chemicals were said to be escaping into the Spencer gulf from Whyalla.

Port Victoria, further north, is a little like Edithburgh, dreaming of days gone by. Port Victoria recalls the era when the masts, spars, and rigging of wheat ships rose in geometric patterns off the port, while they were loaded by ketches which picked up grain cargoes around the Gulf. The last to call there was the *Passat*, in 1949, and now the grain trade is mainly a memory — like the Broken Hill Associated Smelters' operations on Wardang Island, off the port. During fifty-five years the company mined over a million tonnes of lime sands on the island, and sent them to Port Pirie. Now the island is being made into a holiday resort and nature

72

Above: The last ship to call at Port Victoria was the barque *Passat* in 1949. Once a busy wheat port it is now a peaceful holiday resort

Below: Corny Point, at the foot of Yorke Peninsula, is favoured by those who enjoy an 'away-from-it-all' holiday

Wallaroo once shipped out thousands of tonnes of copper every year. Now, ships from many parts of the world carry away the grain stored in Wallaroo silos

reserve controlled by Aborigines descended from the original tribe of the area. Nearby Goose Island is an "adventure camp" for the students of Scotch College, Adelaide.

Northwards lies Port Hughes, and then Wallaroo, modestly thriving through its renaissance as a wheat port. A trip round the coastline will have shown you many more places besides those mentioned, such as the monster new conveyor-belt jetty at Port Giles which some critics have condemned as a white elephant, and little places like Wool Bay and Port Rickaby which never ship a cargo nowadays but are ideal for beach-wandering, fish-catching, away-from-it-all holidays. If you criss-cross the Peninsula instead of driving right around it, then you see Yorketown, Maitland, Minlaton and various smaller townships, all with that atmosphere of bland contentment which pervades country towns that have enjoyed many years of prosperity, and still persists despite economic stormclouds.

Port Lincoln, near the tip of Eyre Peninsula, is only a matter of 100 kilometres across Spencer Gulf from Corny Point, but is a drive of about 640 kilometres by land. You would go to Port Augusta, at the head of the Gulf, and then drive southwards again; over great undulating plains of mallee and saltbush, hemmed in by stark ranges, to begin with. One of them is called Long Sleep Plain, a name bestowed by a Whyalla character who enjoyed a lengthy farewell party with his mates, drove his car north, then pulled off the road and slept the clock round. When he awoke he christened the area by printing the name on a piece of cardboard, and subsequently it was adopted by the council.

Farmers from the Flinders Ranges passed this way when they trekked south in search of new land or labour after abandoning their hill farms to the drought, and a descendant of one of them recalls family stories of how, despite ruin behind and uncertainty ahead, their party travelled in almost holiday mood because of the huge open country which made them feel that they were driving through an endless park.

On their way they would have passed Hummock Hill, a blunted cone rising from near the water's edge and named by the ubiquitous Flinders. Or they might have seen a dark, unnamed group of hills rising starkly from the plain fifty kilometres inland. If so they would not recognise it now, because the hills proved to be solid iron ore and one of them, Iron Knob, has been almost completely carted away in the years since 1900. The others, Iron Monarch, Iron Baron, and Iron Prince, are undergoing the same process, with up to six million tonnes of iron ore a year being extracted to feed Australian and overseas blast furnaces. And beyond them, in the Middleback Ranges, there are said to be yet larger deposits.

It began quite modestly in 1900, when The Broken Hill Pty Co Ltd began to extract ore from Iron Knob to provide flux for the silver-lead-zinc smelters at Port Pirie. A little settlement was established at Hummock Hill, and eleven years later the company built a wharf in order to ship ore to Australia's first steel works, at Newcastle, New South Wales. In 1920 the name of Hummock Hill settlement was changed to Whyalla, a name meaning "place of water." But almost the only water to be seen in this arid area is that of the Spencer Gulf, apart from whatever might collect after scanty winter rains or be brought up from bores. Life for the company staff was rugged, and the most vivid recollection of a relation of the writer's, who worked there in 1922, was of all-pervading clouds of red ore dust blown everywhere by the hot winds.

He would not know the place nowadays. In 1938, when the population was still less than 1,000, the company decided to build a blast furnace to process Iron Knob ore at Whyalla, and to develop a deepwater port. In 1940, just in time to build corvettes for the Royal Australian Navy in the second World War, the shipyard was laid down. In 1958, The BHP announced plans to spend $100 million on an integrated steelworks, and ten years later it commissioned an iron ore pelletising plant which will feed Japanese steelworks. A year later, the population passed 30,000.

A fairly small percentage, including children born in the splendid new hospital and attending the lavishly endowed schools, are natives of Whyalla. Most, however, have come to Whyalla from other parts of Australia and from many parts of the world. In 1967, on a January day with the temperature at 47°C and the sky like blue fire, the writer talked to cheerfully amazed English migrants who had flown out from the grey Midlands only a couple of days before. Nearby, a crowd of Italians romped in the tepid waters of the Gulf. The accents and tongues of many countries can be heard on the streets, and craftsmen who learnt their trades in Hamburg, Genoa, Birkenhead, the Ruhr, Copenhagen, Belfast, or Sydney have toiled in the shipyards and steelworks.

The notion of a town founded upon ship-building and iron-founding may give a picture of grim, grey streets smothered with a blanket of smog. Nothing could be further from the truth. Naturally the works and yards are much like those anywhere else: masses of clangorous steel, scaffolding, catwalks, chimneys, scarlet-belching furnaces, and incomprehensible details to which tourists listen with glazed eyes as they are explained by the guides.

But Whyalla itself has an appearance which is almost gay. Between the burning blue sky and the vivid waters of the Gulf the air has a desert clarity, so that all colours seem more brilliant and every contour more crisply outlined. The streets are clean and tidy, and softened by a remarkable amount of greenery.

A man need never leave this city built between the desert and the sea. He may be born in its hospital, be educated in its schools and then in its technical institute, be married in one of its churches, live in one of the homes which the S.A. Housing Trust built at the rate of 400 a year, work for the BHP all his days, buy all his needs from the privately-owned shops and stores, relax in its clubs, pubs, and cinemas or on its beaches and sportsfields, and at last go to rest in its cemetery. The city is a striking tribute to mankind's ability to plan, organise, and build — literally from the ground up.

Whyalla has been hurt badly by the economic recession of the late 1970s, especially the federal government's decision to cease paying a subsidy to shipbuilders. The shipyard at Whyalla, which built Australia's largest ships and oil-drilling rigs, launched its last ship in 1977 and is now winding down.

What copper once was to South Australia, the iron of the Eyre Peninsula is today: a direct source of wealth, an attraction for capital, an inspirer of development. Because The BHP was prepared to exploit the iron, the State government built the pipeline from Whyalla and set a pattern for supplying water to the rest of the State. A railway has been built there from Port Augusta. The whole State benefits from the Whyalla market for labour and produce of many kinds, and from such auxiliary activities as the mining of limesands at Coffin Bay for use in Whyalla smelters. Directly and indirectly, South Australian progress is fertilised by the mountains of ore which rise from the scrub-covered plains.

Their original contours have been carved away by miners who cut them into sym-metrical terraces, giving them a vague resemblance to Aztec pyramids. They are so huge that they dwarf the massive machines chewing constantly at the red rock, but the machines are winning. Unlike the forests of the South-East, this natural resource cannot be renewed. One day the men and machines will depart and leave the eroded stumps of the hills to the silence of the desert in which they stood for so long.

South of Whyalla, the road undulates through country which to the superficial eye is monotonous and sad. Stony earth as red as iron ore itself, the twisting trunks of mallee scrub and its grey-green canopy of foliage, low ground cover of spinifex, speargrass, and coarse shrubs, sand dunes along the coastline and gently rising hills inland — these are the impressions gained if you fly past thinking only of how to cover the distance. Like so much of Australia, it reveals itself only to those who can accept it, and look with slow observance at the myriad minor details of form, texture, and

The steelworks at Whyalla, where the metal from inland hills composed entirely of iron ore is converted into steel that provides Australian needs

colour which make up the immense whole.

The road from Whyalla will carry you about 130 kilometres to Cowell, whose main reason for existence was once the mangrove-fringed lagoon of Franklin Harbour (named, of course, by Flinders, after one of his midshipmen). The little town looks somewhat shabby now, though its long jetty is being used by fishermen who draw up tonnes of prawns from the recently discovered grounds in the Spencer Gulf. And, since the coastal trade fell away, the tiny ports of Arno Bay and Port Neill also have become backwaters to outward appearance, though like Cowell they have a life which is not readily apparent to the passerby. They stand on the coastal fringe of the great wheatlands of the Eyre Peninsula, and have importance to some of the farmers who grow wheat and wool over 7.2 million hectares stretching to the Western Australian border.

Though much Peninsula land is comparatively poor and its rainfall erratic, these factors are compensated for by the gigantic areas in production. They grow more than a third of South Australia's wheat, and have shipped out nearly seven million bushels in good years. Like all statistics, such a figure is hard to assimilate, but it comes to life when you see the Peninsula at harvest time and the golden plains roll away into the distance.

An old photograph of Tumby Bay, on the Gulf coast fifty-two kilometres from Port Lincoln, shows local farmers grouped in front of a square mountain of bagged wheat. It was symbolic of the "new era that had dawned" for the Eyre Peninsula around the turn of the century. Superphosphate was causing the reluctant soil to yield its fertility, and traction engines had taken over the gruelling work of clearing the scrub.

The huge pastoral properties were subdivided into wheat farms, and the building of a railway for sixty kilometres from Port Lincoln to Cummins enabled the farmers to speed up delivery of their harvest. Eventually the railway linked such inland towns as Lock,

Yarding sheep at Tumby Bay on the Eyre Peninsula. The country is typical of that in low-rainfall areas over much of the State

The *Troubridge* was the last of the Adelaide Steamship Company's ships to trade around South Australian coasts. She runs to Port Lincoln, shown here, and Kangaroo Island

Kimba, Kyancutta and Minnipa with Port Lincoln and Ceduna, and the wheat trains puffed around the ranges and across the plains with their great loads of bagged wheat.

The craft of sewing wheatbags is almost obsolete now. Modern harvesting equipment enables a single farmer to reap thousands of hectares, pour the billions of wheat grains from his header into bulk loading bins, and drive them along the dusty roads from his farm until he strikes the highway which leads him to join the queue waiting at the silos. At Port Lincoln, the silos tower over the waterfront and empty their freight into ships which sail in from India, Yugoslavia, Britain, China, and other faraway places.

They are piloted across the enormous harbour which caused early settlers to lobby so strongly for Port Lincoln as the capital of the State. They did not lose their big ideas. Edward Swaffer, son of the town's first policeman, took up 240 km of country along the West Coast, used it and sold it at a profit, then

took up a further eighty km. Price Maurice operated on equally grandiose lines, and added to his holdings by buying stations for 2s. 6d. an acre from settlers who were weary of dodging Aboriginal spears. The Aborigines of the southern Peninsula are a vigorous and intelligent community even in the substandard conditions in which they live today ("We're sick of talking about ourselves so's writer-fellers can go off and make money out of us," one of them told a social worker) and in those days they fought bitterly against the invaders.

But civilisation conquered, and the industrious settlers built a brewery, bakery, schools, hotels, churches and missions of various denominations, and wharves for loading wool into the clippers anchored in Boston Bay. They mined copper at Burrawing and Copperinga, planted a vineyard and for a short time made their own wine, and feasted on oysters from the shallow waters of Proper Bay. This is separated from Boston Bay by the stubby promontory on which a part of Port Lincoln stands, and gained its name because the original site for the township, known as Port Lincoln Proper, was laid out there. But it proved unsuitable for shipping, and the town grew around Boston Bay.

Boston Bay is one of Australia's most spectacular harbours. Its shoreline, rising to steep coastal ranges which reach their peak at Winters Hill above the town, stretches in a huge northward curve terminating in the hooked cape that reaches towards Boston Island. This island, 6.4 kilometres long, lies across the entrance to the bay, and also rises to a rounded peak, so the whole bay looks like an enormous lake surrounded by rolling hills. It is entered by curving channels north and south of the island, which now belongs to the Davis family and is used as a sheep station. It has facilities for a few holidaymakers, who can enjoy the isolation of its island life and its magnificent ocean beaches.

The golden tide of grain brought solid prosperity to Port Lincoln, and improved communications have given it a sizeable share of the State's tourist traffic. Together with Tumby Bay and Coffin Bay, whose landlocked channels cut into the western tip of the Peninsula fifty kilometres from Port Lincoln, the area provides a spacious vacationland. It is a paradise for fishermen, from those who catch whiting off the wharves to those who battle gigantic white-pointers out in the tumultuous waters of the Southern Ocean. The record shark catch weighed 1199 kilograms.

The great stretches of sheltered water are ideal for watersports, and there are more beaches than you could walk around in a day. Just wandering around the wharves, watching the overseas ships being loaded and the prawn and tuna fishermen overhauling their gear, is a good day's entertainment. Inland, over Winters Hill, there is ruggedly handsome country to explore on the way to Coffin Bay. If you're there in

Boston Island, off Port Lincoln, is a sheep station. This old building was once the station homestead. The island also accommodates some holidaymakers, who enjoy its magnificent ocean beaches

Above: Snags, floods and droughts often meant hazardous trips for riverboats plying along the Murray. Walker Flat, shown here, was flooded in 1956 causing great damage (Photo: Jocelyn Burt)

Below: Paddle boats threshed colourful chapters into the story of the Murray River. Here a houseboat is passing through the lock at Renmark (Jocelyn Burt)

Above: Packing crystallised fruit at Berri on the Murray, where early dwellers saw riverboats in many guises (Jim Gully)

Below: Waterbirds thrive in the marshy creeks and reedy shores of the lakes and lagoons of South Australia's unique Coorong (Jocelyn Burt)

The Caledonian Inn at Robe in the South-East was built in 1859. Fully restored to its original splendour, it is now a luxurious hotel (Jim Gully)

Overleaf: The breath-taking Blue Lake at Mount Gambier changes each November from grey to a dazzling blue. The reason is still a mystery (Jocelyn Burt)

Aerial photograph of Port Pirie. Originally a wheat port, it was
made into an artificial harbour for the Broken Hill workings to
ship out their minerals (Steve Berekmeri)

Above: Wilpena Pound in the rugged Flinders Ranges on the edge of the vast isolation of South Australia's outback (Jocelyn Burt)

Below: Near Blinman in the Flinders Ranges. The vast and primitive landscape retains much that has vanished from the modern world (Jocelyn Burt)

Above: The emu, seen here in South Australia's outback, is the second largest bird in the world. They were once hunted for their blood and oil (Jocelyn Burt)

Below: A waterhole near Coober Pedy, the 'opal capital' of the world (Jocelyn Burt)

Cape Bauer, near Streaky Bay on the West Coast, is typical of the rugged coastline stretching west towards the Great Australian Bight

springtime the bushland is rich with blossom and fragrance. Just across the Peninsula, at Sleaford Bay, the ocean explodes against the dark rocks and the huge sandhills; the same kind of sandhills which the BHP mines for limesands at Coffin Bay while holiday-makers swoop down on them on home made toboggans.

An irregular triangle of highways links most main towns on the Peninsula. From Port Augusta you can take the Eyre Highway across the base, and travel through rolling wheat and sheep country to Ceduna. The Lincoln Highway links Port Augusta and Port Lincoln. The most spectacular is the Flinders Highway, from Port Lincoln to Ceduna. It runs behind the coastline of the Great Australian Bight, and links Port Lincoln with Hall Bay, Elliston, Anxious Bay, Venus Bay, Smoky Bay, Denial Bay, Thevenard, Ceduna, Streaky Bay, and other places with names that recall Flinders' great voyage and the early settlers along what became

known as the West Coast. It was once a wild and challenging area "covered with scrub so thick as to suggest dread possibilities."

Nevertheless the settlers persisted. The first impact was made by pastoralists like Price Maurice, who took up huge tracts of territory, but most of the West Coast was conquered in the last third of last century by the sons of Eyre Peninsula pioneers and farmers from other parts of South Australia.

Distance lends enchantment to our pioneering days, but those men and their families endured hardships and deprivations which would appal modern man. Some, like William Denton at Denial Bay, cleared forty-five hectares of mallee and wattle by hand, sowed fourteen and a half bags of seed wheat, and received only 160 kg of wheat in return. Others grew better crops, then saw them die from black or red rust. When at last they had grown a load of wheat or wool, they had to cart it for miles over rocky tracks and hump it into a ketch which called into one or another of the bays. Their main contact with civilisation was through the irregular visits of such little craft. For the sick or injured, medical aid was so impossibly far away that it was not worth hoping for.

But the settlers persisted, and their persistence obliged the government to provide better facilities — such as a police station at Cooeyannia to supplement the sheoak tree to which "refractory blacks" were chained. Jetties were built, steamships called, and the little towns along the rugged coast began to develop. Each of them was centred upon the church, the pub, the general store, the blacksmith, the police station, and the council chamber in which the farmers and other worthies gathered to forge a local government.

Some of the townships have grown larger over the years, with banks and stock companies' offices and a brief row of shops and maybe a motel to mark their progress; others have not changed much since the first blocks of limestone were hopefully mortared together. When the sun is setting along the Bight, and the sea wind is blowing along the empty streets, they seem as isolated as they were a century ago. It was a hard country which developed a hard, enduring people: pragmatic, self-reliant, and generous, like Colin Thiele's "Bert Schulz" who "Makes me feel the steel of yacca/and the supple punch of mallee."

An increasing amount of traffic travels the coastal road. Much of it is heading towards Western Australia, along the bitumen highway which has at last linked the two states together. Other cars contain holidaymakers who are discovering this coast which the ocean has jigsawed into scores of bays and inlets containing sea-scoured beaches. They fish at Venus Bay and Streaky Bay, watch the seals at Point Labatt, and see the Greek fishermen at Thevenard unloading their catches of whiting which will be taken to Adelaide and even further afield. Spacious, windswept, and handsome, the West Coast still has much to offer to those who go to seek it for themselves.

Succulent South Australian whiting, caught by Greek fishermen like this one at Thevenard on the West Coast, end on the dinner-tables of homes in many parts of Australia

4

North to the Ranges

"Start riding to Adelaide, and buy, beg, borrow, or steal horses until you get there," Sir Walter Hughes told young Bill Horn. "Captain" Hughes owned a small copper mine at Wallaroo, on country which had been part of his Watervale sheep station, and on that morning in 1861 he was told of another copper strike at Moonta, ten kilometres away. A rival mineowner had sent a messenger to Adelaide to file a claim at the Lands Office, and had seventeen hours start.

Horn wore out six horses on the 262 km ride south to Adelaide, and beat the other messenger by minutes. At twenty years old, he was rewarded by participation in the huge copper discoveries in the Moonta area, and died a rich man.

In South Australia, the discovery of copper had much the same effect as the gold strikes in other States. The glamour of "land galore" had begun to wear thin, as settlers discovered that land without tenants to pay rents or ample labour to work it, and with the main markets for its produce lying 20,000 kilometres away, tended to be a bush-clad encumbrance.

The community was depressed and almost bankrupt, though the eccentric "Professor" Menges, a German geologist sent out by the South Australia Company, spoke of buried mineral wealth. But by 1838 the mineral output was worth only £300, from the silver-lead mine of which the ventilation shaft still stands on the slopes of Glen Osmond, above Adelaide. Copper had been seen, but not in payable quantities.

The first to strike it rich were F. S. Dutton and a son of Captain Bagot, who in 1841 found a copper outcrop near Kapunda. They kept it a secret, purchased the thirty-six hectares around it for £80, employed four Cornish miners, and in 1844 sent their first drayloads of copper to Port Adelaide. The effect was electrifying, and prospectors seized with "coppermania" swarmed into the hills.

Numerous strikes proved short-lived, until a shepherd named Pickett chipped a fragment off a rock "as big as a bullock" in the rugged country near Burra Burra Creek, about 150 kilometres north of Adelaide. It was high-grade copper ore; the first manifestation of the great deposits at Burra which were worked for the next thirty-odd years. They were in full swing when the Wallaroo-Moonta mines were opened, and by the end of the first World War the State had produced copper worth 51 million dollars.

Copper had been of immense value in the way that it rescued the depressed little settlement, provided capital for other enterprises, forced new land and sea communications to be opened, and attracted new immigrants — especially the "Cousin Jacks and Jennies" who left the worked-out tin mines of Cornwall for the copper mines north of Adelaide. To begin with they lived literally in holes in the ground, but within a few years they had used South Australian stone to build duplicates of the Cornish villages which they had deserted.

The enduring masonry of their cottages, pubs, chapels, engine-houses, ventilation shafts and bridges can still be seen at Burra and in "Australia's Little Cornwall"; the area in and around Moonta, Wallaroo and Kadina on the root of the Yorke Peninsula.

To begin with, all the copper from Burra had to be taken to Adelaide on bullock drays, and for a number of years an almost continuous procession plodded along the main street of Gawler, which lies near the junction of the North, South, and Little Para Rivers. The township had developed naturally from the camping ground of travellers going north, who found ample wood and water and good pasturage for their stock. The "Old Spot" Inn was built alongside the track which was to become the Main North Road, a smithy and wheelwright appeared, and by the 1840s the town was well established.

It was a vigorous community whose proud citizens claimed that it was the Athens of South Australia. They founded an Anti-Humbug Society to chastise pretenders and the *Bunyip* newspaper in which to publish their forthright views. The *Song of Australia* was sung first in Gawler, when the words by Mrs C. J. Carleton and music by Carl Linger won a prize offered by the Gawler Institute in 1859.

In its commanding position as an "entry port" for the great areas north of Adelaide, Gawler participated in all the pendulum swings of South Australian prosperity and saw the stream of progress pass along Murray Street from its sharply-kinked southern end to its northern bridge across the North Para. The traffic still streams along the same route, but nowadays Gawler is connected to Adelaide by an almost continuous chain of new suburbs. They link the little old town of Salisbury, whose pastoral placidity vanished before the onslaught of new roads and new houses, with South Australia's second "planned city": Elizabeth.

South Australia was the first State to have a town and land planning authority, established in 1920, and made the first attempt to solve the problems of urban sprawl by building a complete new town within commuting distance of the city. The Housing Trust began building the first homes in 1954, and the satellite town was officially opened in 1955. The name of Elizabeth was chosen to mark the Queen's visit.

The first residents along the broad, flat streets had some grumbles about isolation, but the town grew fast. So did the thousands of trees planted in sidewalks, gardens, and parks, and Elizabeth now has a leafy aspect which softens the angularity of its homes and factories and has begun to develop a lived-in look. Many migrants have settled there, and when the shift changes at General Motors-Holden's you can hear the accents of many English cities and counties in the homegoing throng.

South Australia's first large-scale agriculture developed on the plains between Adelaide and Gawler, and three Gawler farmers harvested their wheat with Ridley's original stripper until they wore it out. Land-buyers soon had to look north of Gawler, and when the agent of George Fife Angas began to snap up land there was a rush in that direction. It was good land to settle on: well-timbered and fertile, and receiving a good share of the State's parsimonious rainfall.

Such men as Joseph Gilbert, who bought 1,600 hectares for £4,000, were able to establish splendid estates as the development of overseas trade brought steady markets for their meat, wheat, and wool. As the century grew older they built such splendid homes as Pewsey Vale and Anlaby, and lived a spacious and democratic version of the life enjoyed by the "landed gentry" in their homeland. Gilbert even built his own church, and grew, cellared, and drank his own clarets and burgundies.

Other settlers were content with more modest farms, and nurtured them until they became the countryside which now spreads north of Gawler. It is as fat and well-tended as its own sheep, and in springtime it seems to breathe fertility. Pleasant townships like Greenock, Freeling, Lyndoch, and Kapunda, which are rich in colonial history and colonial architecture, supply whatever the farmers cannot grow in their own soil, and the whole district was seminal in many ways. The sons of its settlers learnt the art and craft of agriculture on its prosperous downlands, and then used their skills to open up new country further afield.

Some of them were among the first students at the Agricultural College when it was opened at nearby Roseworthy in 1883. Other descendants of the settlers carved niches in Australian politics, commerce, and the arts. One of them is Geoffrey Dutton, the poet, publisher, and author who lived at Anlaby until he sold the old house and its contents in 1978.

A number of the pioneers who headed north along Gawler's Murray Street spoke in the rolling gutturals of northern Germany. They were members of the Lutheran migration caused by their refusal to accept King Friedrich Wilhelm III's attempt to combine the Lutheran Church with the State Church, and like their compatriots who had settled in the Adelaide Hills they had been helped by George Fife Angas.

Through the unauthorised action of his agent, Angas found himself the embarrassed possessor of 11,000 hectares of land in the area which Colonel Light had named Barossa Valley, and in 1842 the first 117 Germans settled at Bethany. Further groups followed, and established tiny villages at places to which they gave such names as Gnadenfrei, Krondorf, Kaiser-Stuhl, and Schonborn. The chauvinism of the first World War caused most of the German names to be changed for Aboriginal words.

These miners' cottages at Burra preserve a strong flavour of the Cornish homeland. Many Cornish miners came to work South Australian copper mines from the 1840s onwards

The main street of Burra, a beautifully preserved colonial township which knew its heyday during the region's copper boom which ended in 1877

The valley is that of the North Para River, which winds its narrow way down from the hills and is fed by a complex of creeks. Perhaps it needs the eye of a surveyor such as Colonel Light to perceive that it is a valley at all, for the casual visitor might be forgiven for thinking that it was simply a remarkably pleasing prospect of low, rounded hills through which the roads wind to Nuriootpa, Angaston, Seppeltsfield, Marananga, Tanunda, and the other trim townships.

Their first settlers were not wholly German, for a good many Britons found the countryside to their liking, but the German flavour is strong and pervasive and is proudly preserved by descendants of the early Lutherans. These, incidentally, were as stiff-necked towards each other as they had been to Friedrich Wilhelm. They divided into various sub-sects of the Lutheran creed, and in 1868 a large number of them departed in a huff for New South Wales.

Thirty years before that, young Johann Gramp arrived in South Australia from Silesia. As an employee of the Company he worked on Kangaroo Island, then helped to build the Port Adelaide wharves. After this he became a baker for a couple of years before taking up land near Adelaide, and in 1847 he moved to the Barossa Valley. He settled at Jacob's Creek, and cleared land for a vineyard. Three years later he made his first wine, a white wine of hock type, and the Barossa wine industry was born.

Gramp was not the first to grow wine in South Australia. That honour belongs to John Reynell, whose Reynella vineyards and winery still flourish to the south of Adelaide. He was followed closely by Dr Rawson Penfold, who began to produce red wines for medicinal purposes. His name is seen nowadays on countless bottles of fine wine of every type.

Nor is the Barossa Valley the only part of the State to produce wine. You can stand in Adelaide suburbs and see vineyards terraced

Most of Australia's finest wine originates in the Barossa Valley, north of Adelaide. The valley was named by Colonel Light after Barrosa, the 'Hill of Roses', where he fought in the Peninsular War

across almost perpendicular slopes in the hills, then drive a few kilometres and see wine being made in wineries which now are almost surrounded by suburban homes.

There are vineyards and wineries in Happy Valley, and the old winery of the Hardy family bottles splendid vintages from the grapes of McLaren Vale. Wine is made as far to the south-east as Coonawarra, as far north as Renmark, and as far north-west as Clare, Watervale, and Seven Hill — where the Jesuit Brothers have been making wine since 1859. The diversity of soil types, from the deep red loam of Coonawarra to the limy soil of Clare, produces a range of wines from delicate whites to hearty reds.

But the wine industry is focused upon the Barossa Valley and the Barossa Range. In this rather small area, only about thirty kilometres from Lyndoch in the south to Nuriootpa and Angaston in the north, and less than that from Seppeltsfield in the west to Angaston and Keyneton in the east, with some outlying points such as Eden Valley and Springton, the bulk of Australian wine is made.

In the Barossa, the winemakers work their magic with an almost infinite variety of the four basic elements: vinestocks, sunshine, soil, and rainfall. The neatly arrayed vineyards grow in many different types of soil, from heavy loams to light sandy earth, and present many different aspects to the sun. Some, on the gentle slopes of the Valley itself, receive sunlight from dawn to dusk. Others, on the steep slopes of the hills, may be shaded for part of the day. Some grapes are fattened with sixty centimetres of rainfall a year; others make do with forty. Those on the upper slopes may come to maturity as much as a month later than those in sheltered folds of the Valley.

All these matters must be judged by those who make the wines of Barossa Valley, in the score or so of wineries, large and small, which stand among its vineclad hills. For many Barossa folk, grapegrowing and winemaking are hereditary skills. Their crafts are informed by countless subtle nuances of the kind which such communities know through a kind of osmosis, and which newcomers find so hard to learn.

The Barossa Valley and Hills grow other things besides grapes. There are successful orchards and small farms, but a visitor can never doubt that the grape is king. His palaces are the splendid wineries built over the past century, such as the huge Chateau Tanunda, and Chateau Yaldara, and Seppeltsfield. These, and others, have an imperial magnificence, but of equal importance are the trim homes which stand among the vineyards. They house families who tend vines which may have been planted by their great-grandparents, and who nurture the grapes towards that crucial and anxious moment when they are ready to surrender their juices to the winemaker.

Most places in the Valley have a close link with the past. Samuel Smith's Yalumba vineyard was planted in 1849, and Joseph Seppelt followed two years later. The Salter family's vineyard at Angaston produced its first Saltram vintage in 1861, and Gramp's Orlando winery stands less than a mile from the spot where Johann planted his first vines. Houses, churches, wineries — even some of the great hogsheads which repose in the cellars — are all tangible memorials of the days when most Valley folk spoke German.

Though it is an industry of great commercial importance, winemaking has a tempo and tradition which can be felt throughout the Valley. Wine cannot be hurried to maturity, and this basic fact seems to be reflected in the easygoing dignity of Valley folk and in the massive structure of Valley buildings, from the wineries to the churches.

The Lutherans were great churchbuilders, and their faith still underpins a life style which over 130 years has matured into a full-bodied blend of German and Australian. More Australian than German now, perhaps, but enough has remained of the old customs

Seppeltsfield Winery, in the Barossa Valley, is one of numerous splendid wineries established by families whose names are synonymous with great Australian wines

and turns of speech to give Valley life a savour as rich as the German sausages which it introduced to South Australia.

While the first of these were hanging in the smokehouse rafters, E. B. Gleeson was selling off blocks from the land he had purchased about 100 kilometres north. He had named the district Clare, after his birthplace in Ireland, and in 1868 a municipal corporation was proclaimed under the same name. During the thirty years which passed after Gleeson settled there, the township became the centre of a rich and cultured farming area. The heavily timbered hills and valleys, well watered and profuse with feed, exerted a powerful attraction on men attuned to the soil, and the records of early settlers show that many had been farmers or gardeners in Britain before they took up land in what has now become known as the Lower North of South Australia.

Though it is the smallest of the six divisions of the State it is also one of the richest, and its 2.25 million hectares are closely settled with properties producing wool, wheat, milk, and grapes. Some of them, like that of the Hawker family at Bungaree, are showplaces, and demonstrate in their well-kept land and buildings the loving care of those to whom agriculture is almost a religion.

Others are more workaday, and naturally the Lower North has its share of sloppy farmyards and weedgrown pastures, but the overall impression is that of land which has been contentedly tamed to the service of mankind. Apart from Clare, it contains numerous small towns which come close to it in size: Gladstone, Jamestown, Crystal Brook, and others. And there is a scattering of smaller communities of which some, like Auburn, are as pretty as English villages, while others have an unfinished and semi-derelict look as though the first great impulse of settlement did not survive its early promise.

The district has its share of links with early colonial history. Some are tangible, like

German dancing at the Barossa Valley Vintage Festival. Many Valley people are descended from German settlers and they proudly preserve old German customs and traditions

These wheat fields at Snowtown, with the rounded ranges of the Lower North on the horizon, are characteristic of the many thousands of hectares of South Australian grainlands

the old stone buildings of Clare and other towns; and the "miniature cathedral" of Saint Aloysius at the Seven Hill Monastery. Mintaro, which was established by Cornish miners who bought land there after a successful foray to the Victorian gold diggings, is said to have been named by Spanish muleteers imported to transport copper from Burra to Port Wakefield.

Crystal Brook was named by Edward John Eyre, the explorer, and Gulnare was the name of a dog which trotted behind John Horrocks on his ill-fated exploration of the Upper North. The time to see Gulnare is when the wheat is green. Its tall silo stands on a plain sloping down from the hills, and is the focal point of miles of wheat. When the wind blows across the wheat it moves with an endless sighing rustle, and shimmers in the sunlight like watered silk.

The rounded ranges of the Lower North rise rather abruptly from a broad coastal plain, which also provides good wheatland.

It is fringed, around Port Gawler and up the eastern shores of St Vincent and Spencer Gulfs, by a somewhat indistinguished shoreline: low, flat, and with a tendency to mud and mangroves. If you wish to swim off its beaches you may have to paddle a long way before you are out of your depth. But it is beloved by fishermen, who can spend dreamy days out on its comparatively sheltered waters.

The coast has five ports, all founded on wheat or copper, but Port Wakefield and Port Germein are all but moribund. The former's old wharf, where ketches were once loaded with copper ore or wheat, now provides a rough-and-ready marina for weekend boatlovers. Wallaroo, where the copper smelters flamed for many years, now ships wheat and barley.

Port Broughton, on its deep and mangrove-fringed inlet, is finding a new life as a "play port," and quite a number of its old houses and cottages have been bought as holiday homes. It was a thriving centre in the days when coastal ketches carried much of South Australia's trade. As a holiday resort for farming families, it advertised itself as "the Victor Harbor of the North," though a disgruntled correspondent of the South Australian *Register*, in 1905, complained that "instead of a refreshing dip, I had to put up with mud and mosquitoes."

Port Germein remembers when tall ships glided up the Gulf under a cloud of canvas, and tied up at the great timber jetty, nearly two kilometres long, which was built to stretch out through the shallow waters and enabled them to berth alongside. The arrival of one of them brought visitors from miles around, to watch them load the wheat which would be carried round Cape Horn to the flour mills of Europe.

Nowadays, much of the local wheat that travels by sea is shipped from Port Pirie, of which the *Cyclopaedia of South Australia* said in 1909: "Being so perfectly flat, the town cannot be seen for the houses." Much the same applies today, and as you drive towards the town a first impression is of a forest of television aerials. Beyond them, however, rise the massif of the wheat silos and the dark, smoky complex of the world's biggest lead smeltery.

Port Pirie is one of the State's most important industrial areas outside Adelaide, because it happened to be the nearest ocean outlet when the mines of Broken Hill began to pour forth lead, silver, and zinc. Originally the town had been a wheat port, carved with some difficulty out of a swampy inlet, but it was soon made into an artificial harbour big enough to handle "mountains of coal, lumber, and machinery" for the Broken Hill workings and to ship out their minerals.

Smelting began there in 1889 and has been going on ever since, in a smoky suffusion of prosperity which enables the citizens of Port Pirie to toss around complacent superlatives. Until the recent recession, Port Pirie shipped or smelted more than a million tonnes of lead concentrates each year. The Broken Hill Associated Smelters Pty Ltd converted more than 300,000 tonnes per annum into refined lead, sulphuric acid, silver, gold, lead alloys, copper, and cadmium. A mountain of slag, built up over the years, is estimated to contain six million

tonnes, and a new smelter is hard at work reprocessing this material. It is said to contain at least a million tonnes of zinc. 6.5 million dollars have been spent on port improvements over the last ten years. The grain silos can hold an astronomical number of bushels. And so on. The most recent superlative is the nation's longest railway platform, opened in 1969 to accommodate the Trans-Australian expresses. The rail link from Adelaide, aboard one of the South Australian Railways' comfortable new trains, is a good way to see the countryside of the Lower North.

The Upper North begins a little way above Port Pirie and its 3.95 million hectares stretch to Longitude 31. Above this is what the Government Statistician used to term the Remainder of the State: about 8 million hectares which hold less than one per cent of its population.

The smoking chimneys of Port Pirie are duplicated more mildly by those of the Port Augusta power station, about eighty kilometres north of the great smelters. The power station was built to turn the coal of Leigh Creek, in the Flinders Ranges, into the electricity which marching pylons carry to many South Australian homes and industries. Its smoke drifts across Spencer Gulf towards the steep, flat-topped ranges which rise from its western shore.

Here, the Gulf becomes so narrow that it can be crossed by a bridge, and towards the end of last century a shipping channel was deepened so that steamers could call at the wharves of Port Augusta. It is rare for a ship of any size to lie alongside now, but Port Augusta is still the communications centre for the west and north of the State. The posts and wire for the Overland Telegraph were landed here in the 1870s, and then the railway iron for the tracks which eventually were to reach to Perth and Alice Springs.

There is an adventurous atmosphere of coming and going in this town which lies between the Ranges and the Gulf. Semitrailers go grunting through its streets, laden with machinery for some drilling rig in the red deserts of the north; coaches stop on their way to Perth or Darwin; holidaymakers' caravans sway past en route to Port Lincoln or Wilpena Pound; dust-powdered cars come in from Woomera, Leigh Creek, Alice

Springs, or the Flinders Ranges.

The Flinders Ranges begin in the extreme south of the Upper North. To begin with, they divide it into two very different areas. East of the Ranges, they seem to be no more than rolling hills as you drive north from Crystal Brook, but at last you reach the forested cone of Mount Remarkable, towering above the little town of Melrose, and the road winds around steep timbered slopes on its way to Wilmington and Quorn. From either of these towns you can see the distant ranges of more arid hills, and can visit the rugged defile of Alligator Gorge.

But if you travel by the coastal road or railway, the Flinders show you a sterner face. The slopes which swoop down to the Port Pirie plains gradually become a steep escarpment, frowning at the Gulf across an undulating plain of low, dark scrub.

Port Augusta is linked with the Ranges by two roads, almost equally steep. One winds up to Quorn through the Pichi-Richi Pass; the other to Wilmington through Horrocks'

Pass. They are both exciting scenic drives, curving between huge sugarloaf hills and giving birdseye views across and down the Gulf as far as the distant smoke of Whyalla, but the Pichi-Richi Pass is a railway addict's delight. It crosses and recrosses the line to Quorn, with its steep grades, deep cuttings, stone bridges, and Meccano-like trestles. The line was once to be the start of the railway to Alice Springs and Darwin, and it was said that Quorn would become the "railway centre of the continent."

But it was decided to build another line west of the Ranges, and Quorn decayed until it became almost a ghost town. Its grandiose railway station is deserted, and there are empty shops and houses on its streets, but the town is being revived by the tourist trade. A portion of the railway has been restored by local volunteers, who now enjoy the thrill of steaming an old train up through Pichi-Richi Pass. It has become one of the tourist attractions of the area.

Tourism is the fourth large-scale industry

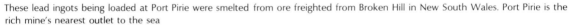

These lead ingots being loaded at Port Pirie were smelted from ore freighted from Broken Hill in New South Wales. Port Pirie is the rich mine's nearest outlet to the sea

Pichi-Richi Pass, one of the main entrances to the Flinders Ranges, is travelled by countless citydwellers each year as they seek the peace and beauty of the Ranges

to implant itself in the Flinders Ranges, and in the long run may prove to be the most successful. However, like its predecessors, it will have its own destructive impact upon the serene magnificence of this area.

The first invaders were the pastoralists of the 1850s: greedy like all pioneers for the land which then seemed endless. Their sheep and cattle ate out much of the natural herbage and died in prolonged droughts, but a number of the station-owners managed to battle on and their successors do so to this day. Next came the copper miners, who with immense labour carted their gear through the rocky valleys, dug and blasted the ore from the hillsides, and have left their memorials in the shape of roofless stone cottages, abandoned boilers, and cascades

of spoil. One of their mines, the Prince Alfred, which was opened in the 1860s, is now being reworked by a group which uses modern methods to extract copper unattainable by even the determined Cornishmen.

Next, despite the longstanding warning by Surveyor-General George Goyder that the rainfall could not be depended on, a rush of wheatfarmers invaded the Flinders. They established tiny settlements which now stand in ruins, ploughed the soil and planted their seed, and for a little while enjoyed good harvests. But Goyder's prediction was fulfilled, and they were forced to abandon the area after their ploughs had eroded the Willochra Plain and destroyed great areas of natural bushland.

For a long time after that, the Flinders were the exclusive preserve of artists like Sir Hans Heysen, and others who loved their ancient peace and beauty enough to make the long, arduous trip into their rugged hills. The Angorichina Hostel was built for tubercular soldiers, in the hope that the dry, clean air would cure lungs which responded to no other treatment, and later the Wilpena Chalet opened in Wilpena Pound and attracted holidaymakers. Now that the automobile explosion of the last three decades has made it possible for more and more people to roam further afield, an increasing number have begun to travel into the Flinders Ranges. Eventually they will have destroyed the very thing which they seek: the space, serenity, and natural wildness.

But for the time being the Flinders can take a fair amount of punishment. No one can blame those who take advantage of the improved road which runs across the Willochra Plain from Quorn to the old rail-head town of Hawker, and then past Wilpena Pound to the mining village of Blinman, and on to the motel and caravan park at Arkaroola — whose owners are trying to conserve the atmosphere and wild life of the surrounding country.

Few casual visitors penetrate farther than that, and even on such a comparatively short

Arkaroola Waterhole, in the Arkaroola–Mount Painter Sanctuary. Founded in 1965, the sanctuary preserves native flora and fauna in the northern Flinders Ranges

trip they will have drunk their fill of distances encompassed by range after range of stark and rugged mountains. Sun and shadow cause them to pass imperceptibly through a whole spectrum of colours. Those near at hand seem to be painted, as the Aborigines believed, with the reds and ochres which the mythical giant Wiltana splashed across them when he made the Ranges. Those in the distance fade into blues which can be astonishingly vivid in certain conditions of light, or gauzily insubstantial at other times, or remote and sombre when the sun declines.

The Flinders have great stretches of park-like country, too, like that within Wilpena Pound. This strange and almost bowl-like formation, enclosed within encircling ranges, contains huge trees which grow on its rolling floor. Great gum trees also grow along the rocky creeks which wind down out of various parts of the Ranges, dry for much of the year, but torrential when flash floods are caused by storms amongst the peaks. When rain does come, it makes the red earth spring to life with huge displays of wildflowers. It enlivens the bush and gums which at other times wait with gnarled patience in the valleys and gorges, and the forests of native pine that give to some areas an almost alpine look, as though one day they will be covered with snow.

Despite the cars and caravans, the trail bikes and the soft drink cans, the Flinders still retain the elemental wildness of antique Australia. Most evidences of human occupation have either a somewhat temporary look, or an appearance of abandonment and defeat. Hawker is dwarfed by the dark ranges above it, the homesteads of sheep stations are isolated on their plains or hillsides, the roofless cottages of long-dead settlers have an unutterable loneliness. Once you are away from the main road and the tiny establishments of mankind, you enter an immensity which offers beauty and escape. The beauty is that of stripped contours and primal colours; the escape is from the myriad minor pressures of urban life, into the basic wildness where humanity can find a cure for many of its ills.

A scene near Blinman in the Flinders Ranges. Despite the invasion by more than 70,000 holidaymakers each year, the region still retains the elemental wildness of antique Australia

5
Where the Bitumen Ends

"We walked on and on. The heat in the day was dreadful and the cold at night terrible. We just kept going, and started having fantasies about waterfalls, full bottles of drink and oranges."

This is not from the diary of a nineteenth-century explorer, but from the Adelaide *Advertiser* report of the ordeal of Dr and Mrs H. Veness in August 1971. They were driving through the South Australian outback to Birdsville, which is just across the Queensland border, but were obliged to abandon their vehicle on a little-used track. By good luck, they were found before they died of thirst.

Modern vehicles and communications have not robbed the outback of its dangers. It is too big. In South Australia, the area which may be regarded as "outback" occupies far more than half of the State. On a good map it has a deceptively busy air, with plenty of creeks, lakes, mounts, tracks, and other features clearly marked. Some of them have fascinating names, like Lake Caddibarrawirracanna and Altukurlpy-klurply. The contour lines, patches of blue, and other geographers' marks give an appearance of an occupied and well-known land.

The reality is different. Once you are away from the very few well-travelled roads you revert to a primitive state in which you depend utterly upon yourself and what you carry with you. Except by chance, you will not see anyone else as you surmount one low, stony ridge after another, cross gibber plains hemmed in by barren ranges, climb red sandhills, and stare across seemingly endless stretches of mulga scrub.

Usually it is silent and dry: so silent that a solitary man can hear the beating of his heart; so dry that the air is like a lens, making distant horizons seem close and turning the night sky into an overwhelming glory of stars. In summer, the heat can be terrifying. You can feel the juices leaving your body, and picture yourself as a parchment-wrapped skeleton.

Sometimes it rains. The average annual rainfall is twenty centimetres, which may be concentrated into a few tumultuous weeks. Then, the blue lines on the map begin to have some meaning. Usually they are only stony, winding depressions, perhaps marked by trees ranked along them and living upon remnants of moisture. But when rain clouds tower over the eroded ranges, and thunder booms colossally over the plains, the water begins to run down the creeks. A trickle at first, then a flood, tumbling in brown torrents towards lakes which until then have been glistening sheets of salt, clay, and gypsum. The waters may even fill them, as Lake Eyre is sometimes filled by water which comes from as far away as Queensland. For the last few years it has contained enough water to support a boat, and for waves to be blown across it and slap on its low cliffs, but there are signs that it is drying up again.

The ranges shine red with rain; the dark scrub crouches beneath it and the red earth becomes so sodden and slippery that it balls in a horse's hoof or bogs a vehicle's tyres. When the rain stops, everything leaps into life. Long-hidden seeds explode into flowers; mulga scrub and myall trees shoot glistening new growth; birds, reptiles, insects, and mammals increase and multiply.

But the sun is thirsty, and drinks as much as a centimetre a day. Sooner or later most of the creeks and lakes will be dry again, though some, like Cooper Creek, continue to hold water unless there has been a sequence of dry years. And there are numerous soaks, springs, and waterholes which were the foci of Aboriginal life until they were commandeered by white men.

Some people fear the outback because it seems inimical and aloof. Others are attracted by its primitive beauty. An increasing number are drawn to it out of curiosity or in search of a physical challenge lacking in their everyday lives. There is even a danger that, during the foreseeable future, the outback will become polluted by the same kind of human detritus which fouls the more attainable areas of the Flinders Ranges. Big as it is, it is not inviolate to modern vehicles and aircraft. A report in the *Advertiser* of 16 November 1971 stated that mineral exploration companies were leaving dumps of abandoned machinery, vehicles, and other equipment behind them.

The outback of South Australia is a huge oblong which contains several varieties of country, though they all partake of the qualities which an old drover defined as, "Flies, sand, heat, bad water, no beer, and general bloody uselessness." In its north-east quarter is the area which Charles Sturt described in 1845 as, "A country such as I firmly believe has no parallel on earth's surface." He was writing about the wasteland now known as Sturt's Stony Desert, but he might have said exactly the same about the Simpson Desert, of which 6,900 square kilometres have now been reserved as a National Park.

Another 650 square kilometres of the outback, the Elliot Price Wilderness National Park in Lake Eyre, has also been reserved, and the two parks form a substantial portion of the more than 250,000 hectares which constitute the State's thirty-three national parks. Together with the Arkaroola-Mount Painter Sanctuary in the northern Flinders Ranges they represent the State's best opportunity to preserve the outback in something like its natural condition, which already has suffered to a greater or lesser degree from sheep or cattle stations, miners, prospectors, oilmen, and others.

The pastoralists were the worst offenders. Even though it might need upwards of ten hectares to support a steer, they were able in the early days to lease enormous areas. They soon destroyed the delicately-balanced ecology of the Aborigines, who in many cases became the detribalised serfs of the stations, and their stock nibbled endlessly at the ground cover. It needed only a run of bad seasons for this to vanish forever, thus creating new deserts, and sunbaked ruins show where yet another station-owner "ate himself out." The flocks of wild goats and the herds of wild horses and camels which roam the outback are a livelier and ecologically disastrous souvenir of the early pastoral era.

The story of the cattlemen and their struggles is as romantic as anything which the Wild West has to offer. It is linked not only with stock-raising in South Australia, but with the great cattle drives down the Birdsville Track for the 480 kilometres from the Queensland border to railhead at Marree. When the railway was opened in the 1880s, mobs of up to 10,000 Queensland cattle were driven down the Birdsville Track.

It was a searing experience for man and beast, because the Track led — as it still does — between the Simpson Desert and

Farina, north of Port Pirie, was named because settlers thought it would be the centre of a 'farinaceous' (cereal-growing) area. It is too arid for farming but it was an active silver and lead mining town from 1872 until 1927

Sturt's Stony Desert: waterless, flat, implacable. Countless cattle staggered to their deaths before the government drilled artesian bores along the track, and tapped the "fossil water" which had lain beneath the land for aeons. It still flows, more than seventy years later, and artesian bores help to supply the surviving cattle stations such as Clifton Hills, which owns nearly 30,000 square kilometres along the Track.

The South Australian outback still supports sheep and cattle, but only the most naive newcomer would enter it with the hope of raising fortunes on four legs. Most people who live in the outback nowadays are a very different breed from the leathery stockmen of tradition — who have been replaced largely by Aborigines. They may be geologists paid by an oil company, patiently cross-hatching country which only a geologist could love. Or engineers working in the natural gas plant at Moomba, not far as outback distances go from the ghost town of Innamincka, where thousands of empty bottles lie in memorial to outback thirsts.

"Safari expeditions" of tourists drive the tracks along which Sturt travelled with fading hopes, and the drovers who "drug the whip" after the cattle mobs have been succeeded by the drivers of beef trains; great articulated strings of vehicles which thunder along the Birdsville Track in hours instead of weeks. You are more likely to meet a painter or photographer than a prospector, and the missionaries who braved fearful hardships and isolation in order to bring the world of God to the Aborigines have given way to competent young men of the Department of Social Welfare and Aboriginal Affairs. In 1921, Mrs Beryl Powell of Killalpaninna Station endured days of travel in the back of a buckboard as it struggled over sandhills and gibber plains to take her to the doctor at Marree. Nowadays, the Flying Doctor from Port Augusta would be at her bedside within a couple of hours.

Sand dunes, rocky ranges, and great rolling plains are characteristics of the South Australian outback. Such country covers more than half the State, with an annual rainfall of only twenty centimetres

The dangers of the outback remain. The Veness couple tasted them; the Page family, three years earlier, died of them, dehydrated beside their stalled car. Yet it retains its eternal magnetism for wanderers and adventurers, and these are attracted most strongly to the opal fields at Coober Pedy and Andamooka. The former was discovered in 1915, the latter in 1930, but they have really come into their own since the second World War. Opal is fashionable in the United States, Japan, and Hong Kong, which buy much of the fields' output of about $7 million worth each year. This makes opal into the State's most important mineral export after iron ore, but for some reason the fields have never been exploited by one of the mineral combines. Opal-mining, or opal-gouging as it was once more commonly called, remains a fiercely individualistic process. Some men work alone, others in couples or small syndicates, and they all burrow like wombats in search of the beauti-ful gemstone.

A few have become wealthy, some make a comfortable living, the majority just get by. A good many of those who go there in search of a lucky strike, or because they are tired of city life or have never been able to settle to anything, suffer the traditional fate of such prospectors and end by working for wages for other men. A few let others do the work and bail them up for the proceeds, and there have been numerous robberies — including those of opal-buyers who carry large sums in cash. A fringe element, both white and Aboriginal, scratches a living by "noodling" amongst the opal potch scattered around the mines, seeking opal chips which will bring a dollar or two. They live degradedly, in old cars or humpies.

One thing the miners rarely have to worry about is the flooding of their workings. Coober Pedy, about 650 kilometres from Port Augusta, and Andamooka which is about 320, are among the driest and hottest

99

places in the State. Coober Pedy miners learnt long ago that the coolest place in summer and the snuggest in winter is below the ground, so they have carved out comfortable underground homes. Some of the mines, which rarely go below thirty metres, are not much deeper than the miners' living-rooms.

It is hard to imagine anyone being attracted to Coober Pedy or Andamooka by anything except the hope of fortune, whether dug out of the ground or extracted from the miners and tourists. They are ugly and desolate places, with the ancient face of the earth scarred by the spoil and potch heaps and the scattered, sand-blasted buildings. But the times are changing, and they are no longer "men's towns" remote from the law. They are on the regular tourist track, so that more and more cars, coaches, and trucks stir up the dust along the roads. Andamooka even has a festival and votes itself a queen, and Coober Pedy has motels. They have gone far from the days when tobacco-chewing prospectors plodded alongside their camels, searching for a "show."

The hardships of the arid inland have never deterred prospectors, and although South Australia's outback has not so far yielded such bounties as the gold and nickel of Western Australia, it has offered its own rewards. Gold at Tarcoola in the 1900s, uranium at Radium Hill in the 1950s and at Roxby Downs in 1976, and coal at Leigh Creek from the 1940s onwards have been matched by the natural gas strikes in the north-east. The first discovery, at Gidgealpa, was soon followed by further successful drillings. The flow is so good, and the estimated reserves so astronomical, that it has been possible for the government to contract for the supply of natural gas to New South Wales. The gas flows from Moomba to Sydney along more than 2,000 kilometres of buried pipeline.

The search for oil continues in many parts

Moomba, in the north-east, extracts natural gas from gigantic reservoirs and pumps it to Sydney

An Aboriginal stockman from one of the surviving cattle stations in the far north

of the State, from the waters off Robe to the Queensland border, and has tapped some promising signs — together with useful sidelines such as the discovery of a well of almost pure carbon dioxide gas near Mount Gambier. The shine is taken off most Australian female skins by talc from the mine at Mount Fitton, which together with Gumeracha produces 12,000 tonnes a year; a formidable amount of face and baby powder.

Nowadays, the prospectors traversing the outback are rarely the rugged individualists who hope that instinct and experience will lead them to wealth. They are apt to be teams of expert geologists employed by the government or by huge Australian and overseas companies — including the Americans and Japanese. They use equipment such as the magnetometer flown above the parched earth and rocks, seeking the emissions from buried minerals, and they sound the unseen depths with shock waves from dynamite charges.

Those employed by the government are not seeking only the glamour minerals. They have been foremost in proving the State's reserves of such workaday but important elements as salt and gypsum, and the government has provided the finance to exploit these. They seek, too, fresh traces of copper and ways of getting more out of the old mines at Callington, Burra, Kanmantoo, and in the Flinders Ranges, and are developing sources near Woomera. Unfortunately the lessening of world demand has slowed these operations.

The natural gas plant at Moomba is a good example of modern technology at work in the outback. Construction of the plant involved the transport of many thousands of tonnes of prefabricated steel equipment along a highway driven through hundreds of kilometres of lonely arid country. Now, the plant stands in absolute isolation. The men who work there, for stretches of eighteen days at a time before they are flown home for a break, are absolutely marooned, but they enjoy splendid living conditions and recreation facilities.

Earlier invaders of the outback were mainly interested in one element: water. To begin with, they sank wells and dug dams (one of which unearthed the coal of Leigh Creek) and then it was found that the north and north-east of the State cover part of the Great Artesian Basin. For millennia, rainwater had been seeping down from the Queensland uplands into the pores and crevices of billions of cubic metres of subterranean limestone, and when the first bore was sunk the water sprang up in a lifegiving fountain. It may have been rain that fell when the Pyramids were young.

The water still flows, at the rate of 6,000 cubic metres a day from 160 government bores, besides those on the sheep and cattle stations which still survive. But underground water cannot prevent stock losses on a genocidal scale when water does not fall from the skies, because the cattle starve to death even though there is plenty to drink. Attempts are made to grow feed by using the bore water for irrigation, but usually are defeated because the water is too mineralised or because of blowing sand.

Nevertheless the outback stations battle on for year after year. In a run of good seasons, they prosper. When rain does not fall, the stockmen have to turn a callous eye upon Golgothas of sun-bleached bones and sun-stiffened hides. Survival in this country demands a particular blend of toughness, patience, resilience, hope, and good humour — which may be why the Aborigines make good stockmen.

Some of the white men who possess these qualities have become legends in their own lifetimes, like Elliott Price of Muloorinna Station. With his family, he rebuilt the derelict station and eaten-out pastures into a thriving outback community, and before he died was able to entertain the entourage of Sir Donald Campbell when the latter set his 1963 land speed record on the salt flats of Lake Eyre. Other men, of equal determination and ability, have been conquered by the outback and faded into obscurity. The stations which they strove to establish have been absorbed by the enormous runs which still survive.

The Aborigines themselves run at least one cattle station, at Ernabella Mission on the Aboriginal Reserve in the Musgrave Ranges of the far north-west. The Musgrave tribes were once regarded as the fiercest of the inland Aborigines, but like all the others they were defeated by the invaders and sank into a profound degradation. They were rescued by the devoted missionaries of various denominations, who have realised that prayers and hand-outs are insufficient fare for the spirit of the dispossessed.

The emphasis nowadays, as in other parts of Australia, is on guidance into self-supporting communities, an aim which is supported by the government. It is meeting with varied success, because a people which has been nomadic since the dawn of time is not easily stamped into a routine mould. Len Beadell, the well-known writer on the outback who spent lonely years in surveying and road-building for the Weapons Research Establishment, speaks of seeing a crowd of Aborigines setting out from Ernabella on walkabout, all in holiday mood as they obeyed the ancient instinct to travel their country. The important thing is that they were happy, well-fed, and cared for, but there are still many Aborigines in South Australia who do not enjoy such good fortune. For many of them the great problem is alcohol, in which they find some consolation for the dreary and motiveless lives which are all that modern society can offer them.

South of the Musgraves, the landscape fits Sturt's description of the northern deserts: "as unchanging and forbidding as ever." Much of it is sandhill country, with steep red ridges marching for hundreds of kilometres north from Ooldea. This name is a corruption of the Aboriginal youldeh, which means "a meeting place providing water," and Ooldea Soak was once the only permanent water within a 160-km radius. The tribes from the coast met there with those from the interior, and traded such items as flint, feathers, shells, and ochre. After the white man came, Ooldea Hut was the confluence of trails from Western Australia, Fowler's Bay, and Port Augusta, and in November 1917 it was the site of a more momentous meeting when the track-layers hammered in the final spikes of the Trans-Australia Railway.

Now the diesels rumble past on their way east or west, and Ooldea is another of the tiny settlements on the line which can be seen stretching away over the curve of the world. At Ooldea it enters the Nullarbor, the red plain which runs into Western Australia. The passenger sitting in the air-conditioned lounge of an express can see the Nullarbor around him in a perfect circle just as a seaman sees the horizon on a calm day. Hour after hour, from dawn to after-noon, the scenery hardly changes. Flat red earth tufted with scrub, an occasional tree, now and again a gully showing that rain does fall here sometimes. The only signs of humanity are the tiny groups of houses where the railway fettlers live, with their back doors opening on the desert.

The detailed story of the railway, like those of many other things in the outback, has never been fully told. The achievements are there and taken for granted, while all the human endeavour that lies behind them has been forgotten. Typical of these is the Dog Fence. This 1.5-metre barrier of wire netting stretches for more than 3,000 kilometres from the Bight to the New South Wales border, and protects the 20 million sheep of South Australia from destruction by dingoes. It stretches for much of its distance through country so lonely that the fence is seen only by the creatures of the desert, including the wild dogs which have never learnt to jump and so are kept in the outer wilderness. It was erected, it is there, and it is of great importance because it guards the South Australian pastoral industry. But few people know much about the years of toil which lie behind its creation, because of its sheer remoteness from its eventual beneficiaries.

Huge areas of the outback remain as little known to the average citizen as the whole of South Australia was when Robert Gouger tried to sell shares in the province. Just as the first settlers could not have dreamed of the growth of the State into its present condition, so we who live today cannot imagine what the future will make of the vast empty spaces of our land.

The lonely outback, where you may travel all day without seeing another human being

BIBLIOGRAPHY

Aitchison, D.L: *South Australian Year Books* (various dates) Commonwealth Bureau of Census and Statistics, Adelaide office. Austin, K.A: *The Voyage of the Investigator;* Rigby, Adelaide, 1966. Baillie, P: *Port Lincoln Sketchbook;* Rigby, Adelaide, 1972. Beadell, L: *Bush Bashers;* Rigby, Adelaide, 1971. Bull, J.W: *Early Experiences and Recollections of Colonial Life;* The Advertiser, Express, and Chronicle Office, Adelaide, 1878. Burchill, E: *Innamincka;* Seal Books, Adelaide, 1970. Burt, J: *The Birdsville Track;* Rigby, Adelaide, 1971. Broken Hill Pty Co Ltd, The: *The BHP Builds Ships; The Growth of BHP; Whyalla;* The BHP Public Relations Office, Melbourne, 1970. Carmichael, E: *Yorke Peninsula Sketchbook;* Rigby, Adelaide, 1972. Corporation of The City of Mount Gambier, The: *A Growing City;* Town Clerk of Mount Gambier. *Cyclopaedia of South Australia,* 2 vols, The Encyclopaedia Company, Adelaide, 1906-1909. Dutton, G: *Founder of a City;* Seal Books, Adelaide, 1971. Foord, R.A: *Lyndoch, Gateway to the Barossa Valley;* The Barossa Valley Festival Committee, 1971. General Motors-Holden's Pty Ltd: *Annual Report,1977.* Government Tourist Bureau of South Australia, The: (pamphlets) *Adelaide; Eyre Peninsula; Yorke Peninsula; Kingston S.E; Port Augusta; Barossa Valley; Arkaroola; Flinders Ranges;* The Government Printer, Adelaide, 1970-1977. Hinton, E: *The South East;* Griffin Press, Adelaide, 1971. Lamshed, Max: *The House of Seppelt;* Advertiser Printing Office, Adelaide, 1951; *South-East Sketchbook;* Rigby, Adelaide, 1970; *Adelaide Hills Sketchbook;* Rigby, Adelaide, 1970; *Adelaide Sketchbook;* Rigby, Adelaide, 1967. Langley, M: *Sturt of the Murray;* Robert Hale, London, 1969. Meining, D.W: *On the Margins of the Good Earth;* Seal Books, Adelaide, 1971. Miles, John: *A Richness of People;* Chamber or Manufactures, Adelaide, 1969. Mincham, Hans: *Story of the Flinders Ranges;* Rigby, Adelaide, 1964. Port Pirie, Corporation of: *Port Pirie, South Australia.* Praite, R., and Tolley, J: *Place Names of South Australia;* Rigby, Adelaide, 1970. Pryor, O: *Australia's Little Cornwall;* Seal Books, Adelaide, 1970. Slessor, K: *The Grapes are Growing;* Oswald Ziegler, Sydney, 1963. Smith, J.R: *Australia, A Geography Reader;* Rand McNally, New York, 1926. South Australian Fishermen's Co-Operative Limited: *The South Australian Fishing Industry;* Adelaide, 1970. Teusner, R.E.: *Brief History of the Barossa Valley;* The Barossa Valley Archives and Historical Trust, 1966. Thiele, Colin: *Barossa Valley Sketchbook;* Rigby, Adelaide, 1968; *Labourers in the Vineyard;* Rigby, Adelaide, 1970; *Coorong;* Rigby, Adelaide, 1972. White, M.R: *No Roads Go By;* Rigby Adelaide, 1962. Younger, R.M: *Australia and the Australians;* Rigby, Adelaide, 1970.

PHOTOGRAPHIC ACKNOWLEDGMENTS

Additional photographs for this book were kindly provided by the following individuals and organisations:

Steve Berekmeri: pp. 71, 74 (bottom)

Jocelyn Burt: pp. 42, 51, 53, 57, 60, 61, 65 (top), 85, 86, 87, 88, 90, 94, 95, 99, 100, 101.

Peter Finch: pp. 37, 55 (bottom), 98, 103.

Jim Gully: page 93

Doug Luck: page 55 (top)

Publicity and Design Services, Premier's Department: pp. 26, 52, 56, 59, 65 (bottom), 66, 69, 70, 72, 73, 74 (top), 75, 77, 78, 79, 80, 81, 82, 89, 92.

SAPFOR Australia: pp. 63, 64.

David Wilson: pp. Title page, 9, 10, 11, 12, 13, 15, 17, 18, 19, 20, 21, 22, 23, 24, 25, 27, 29, 30, 31, 33, 34, 35, 36, 39, 40, 41, 43, 44, 45, 46, 47, 48.